ADVERSITY AND ME

SURVIVING IN MOST ODD TIMES, PUSHING MYSELF TO THE EXTREME, AND BECOME BETTER VERSION OF MYSELF

ARYA KIRAN

CONTENTS

INTRODUCTION

Life has a peculiar way of testing our limits, often presenting us with challenges that seem insurmountable. Yet, it is within these very moments of adversity that we discover the depths of our resilience and the true extent of our capabilities. This book is a testament to the human spirit's ability to endure, adapt, and thrive, even in the most unlikely of circumstances. It chronicles a personal odyssey through some of the toughest trials life can offer, pushing the boundaries of physical, emotional, and mental endurance.

From the depths of despair to the peaks of triumph, each chapter reveals a facet of the struggle and the subsequent growth that follows. These stories are not just about surviving but about transforming through adversity, finding strength in vulnerability, and emerging stronger and wiser. The experiences shared within these pages are raw and unfiltered, offering an honest account of what it means to face one's fears, confront personal demons, and rise above them.

The essence of this book lies in its authenticity. It does not shy away from the harsh realities of life but instead delves into them with courage and candor. It is an invitation to reflect on our own lives, to recognize the adversities we face, and to find inspiration in the relentless pursuit of self-improvement. Each setback encountered is not merely an obstacle but a stepping stone towards becoming a better version of oneself.

As you turn these pages, you will find a blend of heart-wrenching lows and exhilarating highs, moments of doubt, and flashes of clarity. It is a narrative that underscores the importance of perseverance, the power of self-belief, and the transformative potential of pushing oneself beyond perceived limits. This book is not just a recounting of personal experiences; it is a guide, a source of motivation, and a reminder that within each of us lies the strength to overcome and to evolve.

Chapter 1: The Comfortable Life

THE DAILY GRIND

Every morning began with the same ritual: the piercing sound of the alarm clock, the reluctant opening of eyes, and the inevitable battle between staying in bed and facing the world outside. The sun would barely be peeking through the curtains, a faint promise of light in a day that often felt weighed down by obligations and routine. There was something comforting in the predictability, yet simultaneously suffocating.

The kitchen became the first stage of the day's performance. Coffee brewed, its aroma a small but necessary comfort. The ritualistic movements of preparing breakfast, packing a lunch, and ensuring everything was in order for the day ahead felt almost meditative. These small acts of preparation provided a semblance of control in a world that often felt chaotic.

Stepping outside, the morning air was a blend of crispness and anticipation. The commute to work was a time of reflection, a moment to mentally prepare for the challenges ahead. The repetitive nature of the journey provided a backdrop for thoughts to wander, for dreams to be revisited, and for worries to be momentarily set aside.

Work itself was a series of tasks, meetings, and interactions that often blurred together. Each day brought its own set of challenges, some expected, others not. There were moments of frustration, when nothing seemed to go right, and moments of quiet triumph, when a problem was solved or a goal was achieved. The constant ebb and flow of demands required a delicate balance of resilience and adaptability.

Lunchtime offered a brief respite, a chance to step away from the desk and recharge. Conversations with colleagues, a walk outside, or simply a moment of solitude became essential parts of maintaining sanity amidst the hustle. These small breaks were like oases in a desert, providing much-needed relief and perspective.

The afternoon often felt like a race against the clock. Deadlines loomed, emails piled up, and the to-do list seemed never-ending. It was easy to get lost in the whirlwind of activity, to become overwhelmed by the sheer volume of tasks. Yet, amidst the chaos, there were also moments of connection – a shared joke, a word of encouragement, a collaborative effort that reminded one of the importance of community and support.

As the day drew to a close, there was a sense of exhaustion but also accomplishment. The journey home was a time to decompress, to reflect on the day's events, and to mentally prepare for the evening ahead. Dinner, often a simple affair, became a time to reconnect with loved ones, to share stories, and to find solace in the familiar.

Evenings were a blend of relaxation and preparation for the next day. There were moments of leisure – a favorite TV show, a good book, or a hobby – that provided a much-needed escape from the pressures of daily life. Yet, the mind was never fully at rest, always planning, always anticipating.

As the day ended and the night drew in, there was a moment of quiet reflection. The routine of the daily grind, with all its challenges and triumphs, had a way of shaping and strengthening. Each day was a testament to resilience, a reminder that in the face of adversity, there was always the possibility of growth and transformation.

CAREER ASPIRATIONS

When I was a child, I dreamed of becoming an pilot, flying on clouds, and exploring the sky. Little did I know that life had different plans, and the path to my career would be far from linear. Adversity has a peculiar way of reshaping aspirations, nudging us towards unforeseen directions, and molding our professional identities in unexpected ways.

During my teenage years, reality began to set in. Financial constraints, societal expectations, and personal limitations started to cloud my idealistic visions. I realized that the journey to a dream career is often riddled with obstacles, and it is how we navigate these challenges that defines our professional trajectory. My aspirations started to shift from the fantastical to the attainable, yet the fire of ambition never dimmed.

Entering college, I initially struggled to find my footing. The pressure to choose a practical and financially stable career weighed heavily on me. I dabbled in various fields—engineering, business, and even psychology—searching for a spark of passion. Each failure and setback seemed like a step backward, but in hindsight, they were stepping stones, guiding me towards self-awareness and resilience.

A turning point came during an internship at a local nonprofit organization. It was there that I discovered a profound passion for social work and community development. The adversity I faced growing up in a marginalized community had instilled in me a deep empathy for others in similar situations. This newfound clarity was both liberating and daunting. Pursuing a career in social work meant embracing a path fraught with emotional and financial challenges, yet it was a calling I couldn't ignore.

The decision to follow this path was met with mixed reactions. Some saw it as noble, while others considered it impractical. I faced skepticism and doubt from those who believed that success was measured solely by financial gain and societal status. However, the adversity I had encountered thus far had taught me the value of perseverance and conviction. I learned to trust my instincts and pursue what felt right, rather than what was expected.

Graduate school was another crucible of challenges. Balancing academics, part-time jobs, and internships was a constant juggling act. There were moments of intense doubt and exhaustion, but also moments of profound fulfillment and growth. Each hurdle overcame, each small victory achieved, reinforced my commitment to this path. The adversity I faced during this period became the forge in which my professional identity was tempered.

Reflecting on my career aspirations, I realize that adversity has been both a formidable adversary and a powerful ally. It has tested my resolve, refined my goals, and ultimately, shaped me into a more resilient and empathetic professional. The dreams of childhood may have evolved, but the essence of aspiration—reaching for something greater than oneself—remains unchanged.

In the context of my career, adversity has not been a barrier, but a catalyst for growth. It has pushed me to explore uncharted territories within myself, to cultivate strengths I didn't know I possessed, and to develop a deeper understanding of my purpose. My career aspirations are no longer just about personal success, but about making a meaningful impact, driven by the lessons learned from overcoming adversity.

As I continue on this professional path, the experiences of hardship and triumph serve as a constant reminder that aspirations are not static. They evolve with us, shaped by the trials we face and the resilience we muster. In the end, it is the journey through adversity that transforms dreams into reality, and aspirations into achievements.

THE TURNING POINT

The day began like any other, but there was a subtle shift in the air, a quiet whisper that hinted at change. I had grown accustomed to the rhythm of my struggles, the ebb and flow of challenges that had become my constant companions. Yet, on this particular morning, something felt different. Perhaps it was the way the sunlight filtered through the curtains, casting a golden hue over the room, or maybe it was the unexpected calm that settled over me as I went about my routine. Whatever it was, I was acutely aware that the tide was about to turn.

I had always prided myself on my resilience, my ability to weather the storms that life threw my way. But there is a distinct difference between surviving and thriving, a difference I had not fully grasped until that moment. As I reflected on the myriad of obstacles I had faced, I realized that I had been so focused on enduring that I had forgotten to truly live. My life had become a series of reactions, each one dictated by the crises that seemed to perpetually loom on the horizon.

It was during a particularly quiet moment, with the world outside my window bustling with its usual fervor, that the realization struck me. I had the power to change my narrative. I was not merely a passive participant in my own life, but an active author of my story. This epiphany was both liberating and terrifying. To accept that I had a choice meant acknowledging that I had, in many ways, been complicit in my own suffering. But it also meant that I held the key to my own liberation.

With this newfound clarity, I began to dissect the patterns that had governed my existence. I saw how fear had often paralyzed me, how doubts had clouded my judgment, and how the weight of past failures had shackled me to a life of mediocrity. It was a sobering realization, but it was also the catalyst I needed to initiate change. I understood that transformation was not an overnight process; it required patience, self-compassion, and a willingness to confront the parts of myself that I had long ignored.

I started small, setting intentions rather than goals. I allowed myself to dream again, to envision a future that was not solely defined by adversity. Each day, I took deliberate steps towards reclaiming my agency. I sought out new experiences, engaged with people who inspired me, and immersed myself in activities that reignited my passion for life. As I did, I noticed a shift in my perspective. Challenges did not disappear, but my response to them evolved. I began to see obstacles as opportunities for growth rather than insurmountable barriers.

This turning point was not marked by a single, dramatic event but by a series of subtle, yet profound, changes. It was in the quiet moments of introspection, the small victories, and the gradual building of self-belief that I found my strength. I learned that adversity, while undeniably a part of my story, did not have to define its entirety. I could write new chapters, filled with resilience, hope, and a renewed sense of purpose.

As I continue to navigate the complexities of life, I carry with me the lessons from that pivotal moment. It serves as a reminder that within every challenge lies the potential for transformation, and within every struggle, the seeds of growth.

DECISION TO LEAVE

As I stood at the crossroads of my life, the weight of my past decisions bore heavily upon my shoulders. The familiar surroundings, once a source of comfort, now felt like chains that held me back. Every corner of the town whispered memories of struggles, triumphs, and the unending cycle of hope and despair. It was a place that had shaped me, yet it was also a place that confined me.

The decision to leave was not one born out of impulse but a culmination of countless sleepless nights and introspective days. I had to confront the reality that staying meant stagnation. Each day felt like a replay of the last, with no room for growth or new opportunities. The very essence of the town seemed to resist change, and I found myself yearning for something more, something different.

Reflecting on the moments that led to this decision, I realized how much I had evolved. The adversities I faced had carved out a resilience within me, a resilience that now demanded a new stage to be tested. The familiar had become a comfort zone, but one that was increasingly suffocating. I needed to breathe new air, to challenge myself in ways that the confines of my current environment could no longer offer.

There was a deep-seated fear of the unknown, a fear that leaving might strip away the identity I had built over the years. But there was also a burgeoning hope, a hope that leaving could lead to rediscovery and renewal. The duality of fear and hope waged a silent battle within me, each moment pushing me closer to a decision that felt both inevitable and terrifying.

Conversations with friends and family were a mix of encouragement and caution. Some understood the need for change, while others clung to the belief that stability equaled happiness. Their words echoed in my mind, a cacophony of conflicting advice that only I could decipher. In the quiet moments of solitude, it became clear that this was a path I had to walk alone, guided by my own convictions and aspirations.

The day I packed my bags, there was a sense of finality, but also liberation. Each item I placed in my suitcase was a symbol of my past, but also a token of the journey ahead. The act of leaving was not just a physical departure, but a metaphysical one. It was an assertion of my will to seek out new horizons, to allow myself the possibility of failure and the promise of growth.

As I took one last look at the town that had been my world, I felt a mixture of gratitude and sorrow. Gratitude for the lessons learned, and sorrow for the comfort I was leaving behind. But within that sorrow was a seed of excitement, a spark that had been dimmed by routine and familiarity. That spark was now igniting a flame, propelling me forward into the unknown with a heart full of courage and a mind ready to embrace whatever lay ahead.

The decision to leave was not just a step away from the past, but a step toward a future brimming with potential. It was a testament to my resilience, a declaration that I was ready to face new adversities and emerge stronger than before.

FAREWELL TO SECURITY

The moment I realized that security was an illusion was a turning point in my life. Up until then, I had clung to the idea that stability was something tangible, something I could hold onto like a life raft in a stormy sea. But the truth, as stark and unyielding as it was, revealed itself slowly, peeling away my preconceived notions layer by layer.

I had always believed that a steady job, a predictable routine, and a well-planned future were the cornerstones of a secure life. These elements formed a cocoon around me, insulating me from the chaos that lurked just outside. But as circumstances began to shift, I found that what I had perceived as safety was, in fact, a fragile construct. The more I tried to control my surroundings, the more I felt them slipping through my fingers, like sand in an hourglass.

The first cracks appeared in the form of unexpected challenges—an economic downturn, a health scare, a personal loss. Each event struck like a hammer, chipping away at the foundation I had so meticulously built. It was disconcerting, to say the least, to watch my carefully laid plans unravel. The initial reaction was fear, a gripping, paralyzing fear that made my heart race and my mind spiral into endless what-ifs.

But there was something beyond the fear, an undercurrent of resilience that I had never tapped into before. As the walls of my perceived security crumbled, I found myself standing in the rubble, but not defeated. There was a raw, unadulterated freedom in acknowledging that certainty is a myth. It was a lesson in letting go, in understanding that true security comes not from external factors but from an inner strength and adaptability.

I began to see adversity not as a threat, but as a teacher. Each challenge became an opportunity to learn, to grow, to redefine what security meant to me. Instead of seeking refuge in the familiar, I started to embrace the unknown. It was a process, not an overnight transformation, but with each step, I felt a little lighter, a little more liberated.

The realization that security is not a destination but a state of mind was profound. It shifted my focus from seeking external validation to cultivating inner resilience. I learned to trust in my ability to navigate life's unpredictability, to find stability within myself rather than in the ever-changing world around me. This shift in perspective was not just empowering; it was life-altering.

Reflecting on this journey, I see that the farewell to security was not a loss but a gain. It was the shedding of a heavy, restrictive shell and the discovery of a more agile, adaptable self. There is a beauty in resilience, in the ability to face the unknown with courage and grace. This newfound freedom has opened doors I never knew existed, paths I would have never dared to tread before.

In the end, the pursuit of security led me to a deeper understanding of myself and my place in the world. It taught me that true strength lies not in avoiding adversity but in facing it head-on, with an open heart and an unyielding spirit. And in that, I found a security far more profound than any external circumstance could ever provide.

Chapter 2: Venturing into the Unknown

THE BIG IDEA

Adversity has a way of revealing truths we might otherwise overlook. It strips away the superficial layers of our existence, unmasking the raw, unvarnished core of who we are. In these moments of challenge and hardship, we come face to face with our own vulnerabilities, strengths, and the intricacies of our character. It is often in the throes of difficulty that we discover the most profound insights about ourselves and the world around us.

Reflecting on my own experiences, I can say that adversity has been an uninvited yet transformative guest. Each encounter with hardship has left an indelible mark, shaping my perspective and redefining my sense of purpose. It is in these crucibles of struggle that I have found the seeds of resilience and wisdom, sprouting in the most unexpected ways.

There is a certain clarity that comes with facing adversity. The distractions and noise of everyday life fall away, leaving a stark focus on what truly matters. I have learned that adversity is not merely an obstacle to be overcome but a profound teacher with lessons that are both brutal and beautiful. It demands introspection, forcing us to confront our fears, insecurities, and limitations. Yet, it also illuminates our capacity for growth, adaptation, and perseverance.

In the midst of hardship, I have often found myself grappling with questions that cut to the heart of my existence. What is my purpose? What values do I hold dear? How do I want to be remembered? These are not questions that arise in the comfort of routine and predictability. They emerge in the crucible of adversity, where the stakes are high, and the answers are anything but simple.

Through these reflections, I have come to understand that adversity is a mirror, reflecting both our strengths and our weaknesses. It reveals the contours of our character, highlighting the areas where we need to grow and evolve. It challenges us to rise above our circumstances, to find meaning and purpose even in the face of overwhelming odds.

One of the most profound insights I have gained is the importance of perspective. Adversity has taught me that how we perceive our challenges can fundamentally alter our experience of them. When viewed through the lens of opportunity and growth, adversity becomes a catalyst for transformation. It is no longer a mere impediment but a crucible in which our true potential is forged.

There is a certain paradox in adversity. It is both a destroyer and a creator, tearing down the old to make way for the new. It dismantles our illusions and forces us to confront the reality of our existence. Yet, in its wake, it leaves room for new beginnings, for a reimagined sense of self and purpose.

Reflecting on these experiences, I have come to appreciate the dual nature of adversity. It is a force that can break us, but it is also a force that can make us stronger, wiser, and more compassionate. It is a reminder that even in our darkest moments, there is potential for light, for growth, and for a deeper understanding of ourselves and the world.

PLANNING AND PREPARATION

Navigating the labyrinth of life's challenges requires more than just perseverance; it demands thoughtful planning and meticulous preparation. Reflecting on my own experiences, I can attest that the moments of adversity I encountered were not just tests of endurance but profound lessons in the art of readiness.

In the throes of adversity, it becomes clear that a well-thought-out plan is not merely a roadmap but a lifeline. When faced with obstacles, the first instinct might be to react impulsively, driven by raw emotion. However, I've learned that taking a step back to assess the situation is crucial. It's in these moments of reflection that clarity emerges, revealing the path forward. This initial pause is where planning begins.

Preparation, on the other hand, is the silent partner to planning. It's the behind-the-scenes work that equips us with the tools and resilience needed to face life's storms. I recall a particularly challenging period when my professional life was in turmoil. The uncertainty was overwhelming, and the temptation to make hasty decisions was strong. Instead, I chose to invest time in preparing myself—both mentally and practically. This involved acquiring new skills, seeking advice from mentors, and building a support network. These steps didn't eliminate the adversity but fortified me against its impact.

Reflecting on these experiences, I recognize the importance of setting clear, achievable goals. Goals act as beacons, guiding us through the fog of uncertainty. During a particularly difficult phase, I set small, incremental targets for myself. Achieving these milestones, no matter how minor they seemed, provided a sense of accomplishment and forward momentum. It's these small victories that accumulate, eventually leading to significant progress.

Another critical aspect of planning and preparation is flexibility. Life, in its unpredictable nature, often throws curveballs that can derail even the most meticulously crafted plans. I've encountered moments when my carefully laid plans were rendered obsolete by unforeseen events. In such times, the ability to adapt and recalibrate is invaluable. Flexibility doesn't mean abandoning the plan; it means being open to modifying it as circumstances evolve.

Self-awareness also plays a pivotal role. Understanding one's strengths and weaknesses allows for more effective planning. In moments of adversity, I've found that leveraging my strengths and seeking help in areas where I am less proficient made a significant difference. This not only enhanced my preparedness but also fostered a sense of collaboration and shared purpose.

Equally important is the role of mindset. A positive, resilient mindset can transform the way we approach planning and preparation. It's about viewing adversity not as an insurmountable obstacle but as a challenge to be navigated. This shift in perspective can be empowering, turning what could be debilitating into an opportunity for growth.

In essence, planning and preparation are about laying the groundwork that allows us to face adversity with confidence and poise. They are the twin pillars that support our journey through life's inevitable ups and downs. Reflecting on my own path, I see how these principles have not only helped me overcome challenges but also enriched my personal and professional life in ways I hadn't anticipated. The lessons learned in these moments of preparation have been invaluable, shaping the person I am today.

FACING DOUBTS

As I sat in the quiet of my room, the weight of uncertainty pressed heavily on my chest, a familiar yet unwelcome companion. The path I had chosen, once so clear and inviting, now seemed shrouded in fog. Doubts crept in, whispering insidiously, questioning my every step, my every decision. Was I truly capable? Had I made the right choices? The self-assuredness that had fueled my progress began to erode, leaving behind a landscape of hesitation and fear.

In these moments, I found myself reflecting on the nature of doubt. It is a curious thing, both a hindrance and a catalyst. While it can paralyze, it also has the potential to provoke deeper introspection, to challenge the very foundations of our beliefs and motivations. I realized that doubt, in its essence, is not an enemy to be vanquished, but a teacher to be acknowledged.

As I pondered this, I recalled the stories of others who had faced similar trials. Their narratives were not devoid of doubt; in fact, it was often their doubts that led them to profound discoveries and growth. It became clear that doubt is an integral part of the human experience, a signpost on the road to self-awareness and resilience.

In an effort to confront my own doubts, I began to engage in practices that fostered self-reflection and mindfulness. Journaling became a sanctuary where I could articulate my fears and uncertainties, giving them form and substance. This act of writing, of externalizing my inner turmoil, allowed me to see my doubts from a different perspective. They were no longer nebulous and overpowering, but tangible and manageable.

Conversations with trusted friends and mentors also proved invaluable. Their insights and encouragement provided a counterbalance to my internal dialogue, offering perspectives that I had not considered. These interactions reminded me that I was not alone in my struggles, that others had walked similar paths and emerged stronger for it.

In the stillness of meditation, I found a space to observe my doubts without judgment. This practice taught me to sit with discomfort, to acknowledge the presence of uncertainty without being consumed by it. Slowly, I began to understand that doubt is not a reflection of my inadequacy, but a natural response to the complexities of life and the pursuit of meaningful goals.

Through this process, I discovered a resilience within myself that I had not previously recognized. Each time I faced my doubts head-on, I emerged with a deeper understanding of my strengths and limitations. It became clear that the presence of doubt does not negate my abilities or invalidate my efforts. Instead, it serves as a reminder of my humanity, of the courage it takes to strive for something greater despite the uncertainties.

As I continued on my journey, I learned to carry my doubts with me, not as burdens, but as companions that challenge and refine me. They became part of the tapestry of my experience, woven into the fabric of my growth and self-discovery. In embracing doubt, I found a new sense of clarity and purpose, a reaffirmation of my path and the values that guide me.

In this ongoing dance with doubt, I realized that it is not the absence of uncertainty that defines us, but our response to it. By facing our doubts with courage and compassion, we open the door to greater self-awareness and, ultimately, a more profound sense of fulfillment.

FIRST STEPS

The morning light filtered through the curtains, casting a gentle glow on the room. As I took my first tentative steps into a new chapter of life, the weight of past adversities still lingered in the corners of my mind. Each step felt like a delicate balance between fear and hope, a dance between the shadows of yesterday and the promise of tomorrow.

Reflecting on the initial days, I recall the overwhelming sense of vulnerability. It was as if I were standing at the edge of a vast, uncharted territory, unsure of where to place my foot next. The familiar comfort of old routines was gone, replaced by the daunting prospect of creating new ones. Yet, amid this uncertainty, there was an undeniable spark of possibility.

The first step often involves confronting the remnants of past struggles. For me, this meant acknowledging the scars left by previous battles, recognizing that they were not marks of defeat but symbols of resilience. It was a process of learning to see strength in vulnerability, to understand that each scar carried a story of survival and growth.

In those early days, I found solace in small victories. The act of getting out of bed, making a cup of tea, or even taking a walk around the block became monumental achievements. Each action, no matter how trivial it seemed, was a testament to my determination to move forward. It was a reminder that progress is not always measured in grand gestures but in the accumulation of small, consistent efforts.

Support came in various forms. Friends and family became pillars of strength, offering words of encouragement and a listening ear. Their presence was a reminder that I was not alone in this journey. There were moments of shared laughter and tears, conversations that provided clarity and comfort. It was through these connections that I began to rebuild a sense of normalcy, finding stability in the midst of chaos.

It was also a period of self-discovery. I began to explore new interests and revisit old passions that had been neglected. Art, music, and writing became therapeutic outlets, allowing me to express emotions that words alone could not capture. Each creative endeavor was a step towards rediscovering parts of myself that had been overshadowed by adversity.

The path was not linear. There were days of doubt and setbacks, moments when the weight of the past threatened to pull me back. But with each stumble, I learned to extend grace to myself, to understand that healing is a process, not a destination. It was about finding the balance between pushing forward and allowing myself the space to rest and reflect.

Looking back, those first steps were crucial in laying the foundation for the journey ahead. They taught me the importance of resilience, the power of connection, and the value of self-compassion. It was in those tentative beginnings that I found the strength to continue, knowing that each step, no matter how small, was a movement towards a brighter future.

In the end, it was not about the speed or the distance covered but the courage to take that first step, to face the unknown with an open heart and a resilient spirit. And so, with each new dawn, I continued to walk, one step at a time, towards a life shaped not by the adversities I faced, but by the strength I found within them.

INITIAL SUCCESS

The first taste of success often comes with a mix of emotions: a rush of exhilaration, a sense of relief, and a burgeoning confidence that perhaps, just perhaps, the struggle has been worth it. I remember vividly the moment I realized I had achieved something meaningful. It wasn't a grand event or a public acknowledgment; rather, it was a quiet, almost imperceptible shift in my own perception.

In the beginning, every small victory felt monumental. Each step forward was not just a step; it was a leap over the chasms of doubt and fear that had threatened to swallow me whole. The initial success was like the first ray of sunlight piercing through a dense fog, illuminating the path ahead and revealing possibilities that had once seemed so distant.

The journey had been arduous, filled with obstacles that at times seemed insurmountable. There were moments when giving up seemed like the only option. But perseverance became my ally. I learned to draw strength from the challenges, to see them not as barriers but as stepping stones. Each setback was a lesson, each failure a teacher.

As I began to achieve small successes, I noticed a change within myself. The self-doubt that had once been a constant companion started to wane. I found myself standing a little taller, speaking with a bit more conviction. The victories, no matter how small, began to build upon one another, creating a foundation of confidence and resilience.

It wasn't just the tangible achievements that mattered; it was the realization that I was capable of more than I had ever imagined. The process of overcoming adversity had unlocked a reservoir of strength and determination. I began to understand that success wasn't just about reaching a destination; it was about the growth and transformation that occurred along the way.

Reflecting on those early successes, I realize they were more than just milestones. They were affirmations of my ability to navigate through adversity, to adapt and to thrive. They taught me the value of persistence, the importance of self-belief, and the power of a positive mindset.

The initial success also brought with it a sense of responsibility. I understood that I couldn't rest on my laurels. Each achievement was a stepping stone, not an endpoint. It was a reminder that there was still much to be done, many more challenges to face, and countless opportunities for growth.

In those moments of early triumph, I also learned the importance of gratitude. I became acutely aware of the support and encouragement I had received along the way. The friends, mentors, and loved ones who had stood by me, offering words of wisdom and acts of kindness, were an integral part of my journey. Their belief in me often bolstered my own belief in myself.

Looking back, those initial successes were pivotal. They marked the beginning of a new chapter, one where I started to see myself not as a victim of circumstances, but as a resilient and capable individual. They were the first steps in a journey of self-discovery and empowerment, setting the stage for future achievements and a deeper understanding of my own potential.

Chapter 3: The Pandemic Strikes

UNFORESEEN CHALLENGES

Life has a way of presenting us with unexpected hurdles, often when we least anticipate them. Each of these moments carries with it a unique blend of frustration, confusion, and sometimes even despair. Reflecting on these experiences, I realize that they are not merely obstacles but rather intricate lessons wrapped in disguise. The unexpected nature of these challenges can shake the very foundation of our lives, leaving us to grapple with uncertainty and doubt.

I recall a time when I was confident in my path, believing that everything was aligned perfectly. It was a period marked by a sense of stability and predictability. However, out of nowhere, I was confronted with a situation that completely upended my plans. It felt as though the ground beneath me had shifted, and I was left standing in a place I no longer recognized. The initial reaction was one of resistance; after all, who willingly accepts disruption? Yet, it was in this very resistance that I began to uncover deeper truths about myself and my resilience.

Navigating through unforeseen challenges often requires a shift in perspective. Initially, I found myself fixated on the problem, allowing it to consume my thoughts and energy. It was only when I began to look beyond the immediate issue that I started to see potential opportunities for growth. This shift did not come easily. It demanded a conscious effort to move past the initial shock and to seek out the lessons hidden within the adversity.

One particular instance stands out in my memory. A professional setback that seemed catastrophic at first glance. I had invested so much time and effort into a project, only to see it fall apart due to circumstances beyond my control. The sense of loss was profound, and for a while, I was engulfed in a cloud of disappointment. However, as time passed, I began to see that this setback was not an end but rather a redirection. It pushed me to explore new avenues, to innovate, and to develop skills I might never have pursued otherwise.

In retrospect, these unforeseen challenges have a way of bringing out qualities we might not have known we possessed. Patience, for instance, is tested and fortified. Creativity emerges as we seek out alternative solutions. Empathy grows as we realize that everyone faces their own set of unexpected trials. These experiences, while difficult, contribute to a richer, more nuanced understanding of life and our place within it.

There is also a profound sense of humility that accompanies the navigation of unforeseen challenges. They remind us that, despite our best efforts, we are not in control of everything. This realization can be both humbling and liberating. It allows us to release the tight grip we often have on our plans and to be more open to the fluid nature of life.

Reflecting on these moments of adversity, I see them as integral parts of my journey. They have shaped my character, influenced my decisions, and ultimately led me to a deeper appreciation of the unpredictable nature of existence. While the initial impact of unforeseen challenges can be jarring, the long-term effects are often transformative, leaving us stronger and more adaptable than before.

LOCKDOWN REALITIES

In the quiet corners of our homes, a new kind of reality began to take shape. The once bustling streets fell silent, and the cacophony of daily life was replaced by an eerie stillness. This was a time of profound change, a global pause that forced us all to confront the essence of our existence.

The walls of our homes, once merely boundaries of personal space, transformed into the limits of our world. The familiar routines of morning commutes and face-to-face interactions were replaced by screens and digital connections. The shift was abrupt, leaving many of us grappling with a new kind of solitude. It was as if the universe had handed us a mirror, compelling us to look inward, to face our thoughts, fears, and aspirations in ways we had never done before.

There was an initial sense of novelty, almost an adventure, in adapting to this new way of life. Home offices sprang up in kitchens, living rooms became classrooms, and every corner of our homes was repurposed to fit the demands of this unprecedented time. However, as days turned into weeks, and weeks into months, the weight of isolation began to settle in. The absence of physical presence, the lack of spontaneous laughter, and the simple joy of human touch became glaringly apparent.

Yet, amidst the challenges, there were moments of unexpected clarity. The slowing down of life offered a rare chance to reconnect with ourselves and those closest to us. Families shared meals and stories, rekindling bonds that had been frayed by the rush of modern life. We rediscovered the art of conversation, the pleasure of a shared silence, and the comfort of being truly present with one another.

For many, this period was a test of mental resilience. The constant barrage of news, the uncertainty of the future, and the omnipresent fear of the virus created a fertile ground for anxiety and stress. Yet, it also highlighted the importance of mental health and self-care. People turned to meditation, yoga, and other mindfulness practices, seeking solace in the midst of chaos. Books became companions, music a refuge, and nature walks a balm for the soul.

The digital realm, once a mere tool for convenience, became a lifeline. Virtual gatherings, online classes, and digital collaborations became the new normal. While nothing could replace the warmth of in-person interactions, technology offered a bridge, connecting us in ways that were previously unimagined. It was a testament to human adaptability and the innate desire to stay connected, even when physically apart.

This period also brought to light the stark inequalities that exist in our society. The privilege of working from home, access to healthcare, and the ability to maintain social distance were not universal. The pandemic exposed the vulnerabilities of marginalized communities, urging us to reflect on our collective responsibility towards each other.

As we navigated through these challenging times, there was a growing recognition of the strength that lies in community and solidarity. Small acts of kindness, support networks, and communal efforts to help those in need became beacons of hope. It was a reminder that, despite the physical distance, we are all interconnected, and our actions have the power to uplift and inspire.

In this enforced stillness, we found an opportunity to reevaluate our priorities, to cherish the simple joys, and to emerge with a deeper understanding of ourselves and the world around us.

FINANCIAL STRAIN

The weight of financial struggles can be an invisible burden, one that quietly infiltrates every corner of life. Money, or the lack thereof, has a way of gnawing at the edges of one's peace, creating a constant hum of anxiety that is difficult to silence. It's not just about the immediate pressure of unpaid bills or the mounting debt that seems to grow exponentially; it's about the pervasive sense of inadequacy that seeps into one's self-worth.

There were days when the mailbox became a source of dread, each envelope a potential harbinger of bad news. I remember the feeling of opening a bill and seeing numbers that felt insurmountable, a stark reminder of the precariousness of my situation. It wasn't just the numbers that hurt; it was the realization that I had somehow failed to manage my resources, that I was not as resilient as I had believed. The shame was a silent companion, whispering doubts and fears that were hard to ignore.

This strain had a domino effect, touching relationships and altering interactions in subtle, yet profound ways. The tension of financial uncertainty created an undercurrent of stress that was almost tangible. Conversations with loved ones became strained, not because of any lack of affection, but because the worry was always there, lurking just beneath the surface. It was difficult to be present, to enjoy the simple pleasures, when a part of my mind was constantly calculating, budgeting, and worrying about the next financial hurdle.

Sleep, too, became elusive. Nights were spent tossing and turning, wrestling with the fear of what might come. The mind, in its relentless pursuit of solutions, would not rest. Each night felt like a battleground, where hope and despair fought for dominance. There were moments when the exhaustion was so overwhelming that it felt like a physical weight, pressing down with an almost unbearable force.

The social aspect of life didn't escape unscathed either. Invitations to gatherings were often declined, not because of a lack of desire to connect, but because of the financial implications. The cost of a meal out, a gift for a friend, or even the gas to get to an event became significant considerations. Each declined invitation was a reminder of the isolation that financial strain could impose, creating a barrier between myself and the world.

Yet, amidst the turmoil, there were small victories and lessons learned. A deeper appreciation for the value of money and the importance of managing it wisely began to take root. The experience fostered a resilience that was born out of necessity. There was a newfound respect for the strength it took to navigate such challenges, a recognition of the inner fortitude that had been lying dormant.

Reflecting on those times, it is clear that the financial strain was more than just a challenge to be overcome; it was a crucible that forged a more resilient, resourceful version of myself. It taught the importance of perseverance, the value of seeking help when needed, and the power of hope. It was a reminder that while financial stability is crucial, it is the strength of character and the support of loved ones that truly sustain us through the darkest times.

BUSINESS DOWNFALL

The weight of the world seemed to settle on my shoulders as I watched the decline of what I had once proudly built. Every entrepreneur dreams of success, but few prepare for the crushing reality of failure. The signs were subtle at first— a missed opportunity here, a dissatisfied client there. But soon, the cracks in the foundation became impossible to ignore, and the edifice I had constructed began to crumble.

I remember the late nights, poring over financial statements that bled red ink. Desperation drove me to consider options I would have once deemed unthinkable. There were moments when hope flickered, only to be extinguished by another setback. Each phone call from creditors tightened the noose around my aspirations. The relentless march of time offered no solace, only a countdown to inevitable collapse.

The hardest part was facing the employees who had believed in the vision as fervently as I had. Their livelihoods were intertwined with the fate of the business, and the guilt of letting them down gnawed at me. Meetings became somber affairs, filled with forced optimism and unspoken fears. Every decision felt like a double-edged sword, cutting deeper into the fragile fabric of our collective dreams.

Friends and family, well-meaning though they were, offered advice that sounded hollow. "Just hang in there," they would say, as if sheer willpower could reverse the tides of misfortune. Their words, meant to comfort, only served to underscore the isolation I felt. The gap between their understanding and my reality seemed insurmountable. It was a lonely descent, marked by sleepless nights and endless self-recrimination.

There were moments of introspection, where I questioned every choice that had led me to this point. Was it hubris that blinded me to the risks? Or was it merely the unpredictability of the market? The answers eluded me, and perhaps, they always will. What remained was the stark truth that my venture, once a beacon of hope, had become a cautionary tale.

Yet, through the haze of despair, there were glimmers of resilience. Each failure taught a lesson, harsh but invaluable. The art of pivoting, the importance of adaptability, and the necessity of humility became clearer with every misstep. The business world, unforgiving as it is, also has a way of imparting wisdom that no textbook can offer.

As the final chapter of this endeavor drew to a close, there was a strange sense of liberation. The end, though painful, brought with it a clarity that success often obscures. Stripped of illusions, I stood face to face with my limitations and my strengths. The business had fallen, but in its wake, a new understanding emerged.

This was not the end of the road, but rather a turn in the journey. The lessons learned in the crucible of failure would serve as a foundation for whatever came next. In the silence that followed the storm, there was space to rebuild, to rethink, and to renew. The path forward was uncertain, but it was mine to navigate. And with each step, the shadows of the past grew fainter, leaving room for the light of new beginnings.

HITTING ROCK BOTTOM

The days melded into one another, each indistinguishable from the last, a monochrome blur of despair and isolation. I found myself standing at the precipice of my own existence, peering into an abyss that seemed to have no bottom. The weight of my failures, both real and perceived, pressed down on me with a suffocating intensity. It was a moment of unparalleled clarity and confusion, where every misstep and wrong turn seemed to converge into a singular, unbearable point.

In this state, the world outside continued its indifferent march forward. Friends and family, despite their best intentions, became distant echoes, their words of encouragement and concern failing to penetrate the fortress of my desolation. It was as though I had been cast adrift in a sea of my own making, the shorelines of hope and solace receding ever further into the horizon.

There was a peculiar kind of numbness that settled in, a protective shell against the rawness of my emotions. Yet, within that numbness, there was also a profound sense of awareness. I could see, with stark clarity, the patterns and choices that had led me to this point. Each decision, each moment of weakness or pride, was laid bare before me. It was a painful but necessary inventory of my life, an unflinching look at the person I had become.

In the quiet solitude of those dark days, I began to understand the true nature of adversity. It is not merely an external force that acts upon us, but an internal crucible that shapes and refines our very essence. The struggles and failures we face are not just obstacles to be overcome, but lessons to be learned, each one offering a deeper insight into our own character and resilience.

There were moments when the darkness seemed impenetrable, when the idea of moving forward felt like an insurmountable challenge. But within that darkness, there were also flickers of light, small but persistent reminders of the strength and potential that lay within. It was in those moments of quiet reflection that I found the seeds of a renewed purpose, a glimmer of hope that suggested a way forward, even if the path was not yet clear.

The journey through rock bottom is not a linear one. It is fraught with setbacks and false starts, moments of progress followed by periods of regression. But it is also a journey of profound self-discovery, a chance to rebuild from the ground up with a newfound understanding of what truly matters. It is an opportunity to let go of the illusions and pretenses that have weighed us down, and to embrace a more authentic and resilient version of ourselves.

As I navigated this tumultuous terrain, I came to realize that hitting rock bottom was not an end, but a beginning. It was a chance to strip away the extraneous and focus on the core of who I am and who I want to be. It was an invitation to rebuild, not just my external circumstances, but my inner world, with a foundation rooted in strength, compassion, and unwavering resolve.

Chapter 4: Odd Jobs and Humble Beginnings

SEARCHING FOR WORK

The relentless pursuit of employment often feels like navigating a labyrinth with an ever-shifting layout. Each turn, each decision, can lead to a breakthrough or a dead end. The process demands not just patience, but a deep introspection about one's own capabilities and limitations. It's a time when the mirror reflects not just the physical self, but the internal strengths and weaknesses that define us.

In the early days, the optimism is palpable. Armed with a freshly polished resume and a cover letter that sings praises of one's own achievements, the initial applications are sent out with a sense of purpose. Each job listing is scrutinized, each requirement matched with a bullet point on the resume, each potential employer researched with the diligence of a scholar. The hope is that this effort will be recognized, that somewhere out there, an opportunity awaits.

But as days turn into weeks, and weeks into months, the optimism begins to wane. Each automated rejection email feels like a personal slight, a reminder of one's perceived inadequacies. The silence from potential employers is deafening, and the doubts start to creep in. Am I not good enough? Did I choose the wrong career path? The once clear vision of the future becomes clouded with uncertainty.

Yet, in these moments of doubt, there is also a chance for growth. The process of searching for work is not just about finding a job; it's about finding oneself. It's about understanding what truly matters, what one is willing to compromise on, and what remains non-negotiable. It's about resilience, about picking oneself up after each setback and continuing to push forward.

Networking becomes a crucial lifeline. Reaching out to former colleagues, attending industry events, and engaging in professional groups can open doors that online applications cannot. These interactions remind one of the human element in the job search, the connections and relationships that can make all the difference. It's in these conversations that new opportunities often arise, sometimes from the most unexpected sources.

The journey also involves continuous learning. In a rapidly changing world, staying stagnant is not an option. Whether it's taking up an online course, attending workshops, or simply reading up on the latest industry trends, every bit of knowledge gained is a step closer to the goal. This commitment to self-improvement not only enhances one's skill set but also boosts confidence, a crucial asset in any job interview.

And then, there is the introspection. The quiet moments when one reflects on past experiences, both professional and personal. These reflections provide clarity, helping to identify what truly drives and motivates. They offer insights into what kind of work environment would be fulfilling, what roles would align with one's values and aspirations.

The search for work is undoubtedly challenging, often testing the limits of one's patience and perseverance. But it is also a transformative experience. It strips away the superficial, forcing a confrontation with the core of one's being. It demands honesty, resilience, and above all, hope. Because in the end, it is this hope that propels one forward, that fuels the belief that somewhere, there is a place where one's skills and passions will be recognized and valued.

LEARNING ON THE JOB

As I navigated the labyrinth of my early career, I often found myself grappling with unexpected challenges that seemed to test the very core of my resilience. Each day presented a new puzzle, a fresh conundrum that required not just knowledge but an unyielding determination to persevere. It was during these times that I realized the true essence of learning on the job.

The corporate world, with its intricate dynamics and unwritten rules, was a far cry from the theoretical sanctuary of academia. Textbooks and lectures had painted a picture of structured problem-solving, but reality was a kaleidoscope of shifting priorities and unforeseen obstacles. My first project felt like being tossed into a tempest, with deadlines looming like dark clouds and expectations crashing like relentless waves. The initial overwhelm was palpable, but it also ignited a spark of tenacity within me.

One of the most profound lessons I absorbed was the art of adaptability. I learned that rigidity was a luxury I could ill afford. Projects often deviated from their planned course, and the ability to pivot, to reassess and recalibrate, became invaluable. It was in these moments of flux that I discovered the strength of flexibility, the power of a mindset that could bend without breaking.

Mentorship played a pivotal role in my professional development. The guidance of seasoned colleagues, their willingness to share their wisdom and experiences, became a beacon in the fog of uncertainty. These mentors were not just advisors; they were exemplars of perseverance. Their stories of past struggles and triumphs offered a roadmap, a series of signposts that illuminated the path ahead. Through their counsel, I learned that mistakes were not failures but stepping stones to mastery.

Collaboration emerged as another cornerstone of my growth. The notion of solitary success was swiftly dismantled by the reality of teamwork. Each project was a tapestry woven from the threads of diverse skills and perspectives. I learned to value the contributions of my peers, to recognize that collective effort often yielded results far greater than individual endeavor. The synergy of a well-coordinated team, the harmony of shared goals and mutual support, became a source of both strength and inspiration.

There were moments of doubt, instances where the weight of expectations felt insurmountable. Yet, it was in these very moments that I discovered an inner reservoir of resilience. The pressure, rather than crushing me, forged a new understanding of my capabilities. I learned to trust in my instincts, to believe in the knowledge I had acquired and the skills I was honing. Each challenge surmounted became a testament to my growth, a marker of progress on a journey defined by perseverance.

In retrospect, the process of learning on the job was not just about acquiring new skills or knowledge. It was an odyssey of self-discovery, a journey that revealed the depths of my potential and the breadth of my resilience. The crucible of professional challenges shaped me, molding my character and fortifying my resolve. Through the trials and tribulations, I emerged not just as a more competent professional, but as a more resilient and self-assured individual.

MEETING NEW PEOPLE

Navigating through the chaos of life often brings us to unexpected intersections with others, each encounter a potential turning point. These moments, seemingly ordinary, hold the power to shape our journey in profound ways. Reflecting on my own experiences, I realize how the fabric of my life is woven with threads of chance meetings and serendipitous connections.

In the throes of adversity, it's easy to recoil, to wrap oneself in a cocoon of familiar faces and places. Yet, it is precisely during these times that new people can bring fresh perspectives and unforeseen opportunities. I recall a particularly difficult period when I felt isolated, my struggles weighing heavily on my spirit. It was then that I met Radha (Name Changed).

Radha was a force of nature, her energy palpable even in a crowded room. Our paths crossed at a community event I had reluctantly attended. Initially, I was hesitant to engage, my mind clouded with the weight of my own issues. But Radha's warmth and genuine interest in others were disarming. She had an uncanny ability to listen, to make you feel seen and heard. Through our conversations, I found myself opening up, sharing thoughts I had long kept buried.

Radha's impact on my life was profound. She introduced me to a network of individuals who, like her, were passionate about supporting others. Through these connections, I began to see my challenges in a new light. They were not insurmountable obstacles but rather opportunities for growth and resilience. This shift in perspective was a turning point, sparking a renewed sense of purpose within me.

Another pivotal encounter was with a mentor, Vikas (Name Changed), whom I met during a professional workshop. Vikas was a seasoned expert in my field, his reputation preceding him. Despite his accomplishments, he was approachable and humble. Our initial conversation was brief, yet it left a lasting impression. Vikas offered insights that resonated deeply with me, encouraging me to pursue my ambitions with renewed vigor.

Over time, Vikas became more than a mentor; he became a confidant and a source of unwavering support. His guidance helped me navigate the complexities of my career, but more importantly, he taught me the value of perseverance and self-belief. Through his mentorship, I learned that setbacks were not failures but stepping stones towards success.

Reflecting on these experiences, I realize that meeting new people is not merely about expanding one's social circle. It's about opening oneself to the possibility of change, of growth. Each new person we meet holds a mirror to our own lives, reflecting back our strengths and vulnerabilities. They challenge us to see the world through different lenses, to question our assumptions and broaden our horizons.

In the tapestry of my life, the threads of these encounters are vibrant and varied. They have added depth and richness to my journey, each one a testament to the power of human connection. As I continue to navigate the ups and downs of life, I remain open to the possibility that the next person I meet could be another thread, another story, another lesson waiting to unfold.

In moments of darkness, it is often the light of others that guides us forward. Their presence, their stories, and their support can illuminate the path ahead, reminding us that we are never truly alone.

FINDING JOY IN SMALL WINS

In the tapestry of our lives, it is often the grand achievements that get the spotlight. Yet, in the shadows of these monumental milestones, there exist myriad moments that, though smaller in scale, carry a profound impact. These moments, often overlooked, hold the power to uplift and sustain us through the rough patches of our journey.

I remember a time when the weight of adversity felt insurmountable. Each day seemed to blend into the next, a monotonous rhythm of struggle and perseverance. It was during one of these particularly challenging periods that I stumbled upon an unexpected revelation: the significance of small wins.

There was a day when, after countless attempts, I finally managed to get out of bed without the familiar dread of what lay ahead. It was a simple act, one that many might take for granted, but for me, it was a victory. That morning, I made myself a cup of tea and sat by the window, savoring the warmth of the mug in my hands. The sun was just beginning to rise, casting a golden hue across the room. In that moment, I felt a flicker of joy, a sense of accomplishment that seemed disproportionate to the act itself. It was then that I realized the power of acknowledging and celebrating these small victories.

The beauty of small wins lies in their accessibility. They are not dependent on external validation or grand gestures. They are personal, intimate, and deeply rooted in our everyday experiences. Whether it's completing a task that has been looming over us, finding the courage to voice our thoughts, or simply taking a moment for ourselves, these wins are the building blocks of resilience.

Reflecting on these moments, I began to see a pattern. Each small win, though seemingly insignificant on its own, contributed to a larger mosaic of progress and growth. They served as reminders that even in the face of adversity, there is always something to be grateful for, something to celebrate. This shift in perspective was transformative. It allowed me to find joy in the present, rather than constantly yearning for a distant, elusive future.

As I continued to navigate the challenges before me, I made it a habit to acknowledge and cherish these small wins. I started keeping a journal, noting down each victory, no matter how minor it seemed. This practice became a source of strength, a tangible reminder of my progress and resilience. It also fostered a sense of mindfulness, encouraging me to stay present and fully engage with each moment.

Over time, I noticed a change in my outlook. The days no longer felt like an endless series of struggles. Instead, they were punctuated with moments of joy and accomplishment. These small wins became a source of motivation, propelling me forward even on the toughest days.

Through this journey, I learned that adversity does not have to overshadow our lives. By finding joy in small wins, we can cultivate a sense of fulfillment and resilience. These moments, though fleeting, have the power to light our path, guiding us through the darkest times. They remind us that progress is not always measured by grand achievements, but by the accumulation of small, meaningful victories.

Chapter 5: Navigating Uncertainty

BALANCING ACT

Navigating through life's challenges has always felt like walking a tightrope. Each step demands precision, focus, and the courage to maintain balance despite the strong winds trying to sway me off course. I often find myself reflecting on how adversity, in its many forms, has shaped the person I am today. There's an almost poetic irony in how the very obstacles that once seemed insurmountable have become the stepping stones of my life's journey.

In the quiet moments of introspection, I realize that adversity isn't just a force to be reckoned with; it's a teacher. It has a way of stripping away the superficial layers, revealing the core of our resilience and strength. Each challenge encountered has brought with it a lesson, sometimes subtle, sometimes stark, but always significant. These lessons have taught me to appreciate the delicate balance between persistence and acceptance.

There were times when I felt overwhelmed, as though the weight of my struggles would crush me. Yet, it was in these moments of vulnerability that I discovered an inner strength I didn't know existed. I learned that balance isn't about perfection; it's about finding harmony amid chaos. It's about recognizing that falling is an inevitable part of the process and that the true measure of strength lies in the willingness to get back up.

Reflecting on past adversities, I see a pattern emerge. Each challenge has pushed me to grow, to adapt, and to redefine my limits. The failures, disappointments, and setbacks have all played a crucial role in sculpting my character. They have taught me patience, empathy, and the importance of self-compassion. Most importantly, they have shown me that balance is not a static state but a dynamic one, requiring constant adjustment and mindfulness.

It's easy to look back with the clarity of hindsight and see how each piece of the puzzle fits together. However, in the midst of adversity, the picture is often blurred, and the path forward seems uncertain. During these times, I've learned to trust in the process, to have faith that even the most challenging experiences have value. This trust has been a guiding light, helping me navigate through the darkest hours.

One of the most profound realizations I've had is that adversity is a shared human experience. It connects us, reminding us that we are not alone in our struggles. This sense of connection has been a source of comfort and strength. Knowing that others have faced similar challenges and emerged stronger has inspired me to persevere.

As I continue to walk this tightrope, I am reminded that balance is a continuous endeavor. It requires mindfulness, self-awareness, and a willingness to adapt. Each step forward is a testament to the resilience of the human spirit and the transformative power of adversity. Through this reflective lens, I see that every challenge faced is an opportunity for growth, a chance to refine the balance that guides us through life.

EMOTIONAL TURMOIL

The days seemed to blur together, each one marked by a sense of disquiet that I couldn't quite shake. It was as though I was walking through a fog, unable to see more than a few steps ahead. Every decision felt monumental, and every interaction seemed fraught with unspoken tension. I found myself questioning everything, from my purpose to my sense of self. This was not just a rough patch; it was a tempest raging within.

I remember the first time I noticed something was amiss. It was an ordinary morning, the sun filtering through the curtains, casting a warm glow across the room. Yet, as I sat up in bed, a wave of inexplicable sadness washed over me. It wasn't tied to any specific event or thought. It just was. I tried to shake it off, attributing it to a bad night's sleep or perhaps stress. But as the days turned into weeks, it became clear that this was something deeper, something more profound.

Conversations with friends and family became challenging. Their words often seemed to come from a distance, as though they were speaking through a thick pane of glass. I could hear them, but the meaning was lost. Even the simplest of interactions felt like a Herculean effort. I remember sitting across from a dear friend at a café, her words a comforting murmur, yet I felt utterly disconnected. It was as if I was present in body but absent in spirit.

Work, too, became an arena of emotional struggle. Tasks that once brought satisfaction now felt burdensome. The passion and drive that had fueled my professional life seemed to have evaporated, leaving behind a hollow shell of obligation. Meetings were endured, not engaged in. Deadlines loomed like ominous clouds, and each completed task felt like a drop in an endless ocean of futility.

Nights were the hardest. Lying in the dark, the silence was deafening. Thoughts raced, each one more troubling than the last. Memories of past failures, anxieties about the future, and a pervasive sense of inadequacy swirled in a relentless loop. Sleep, when it came, was fitful and unrefreshing. I would wake up more exhausted than before, the cycle starting anew with the dawn.

Seeking solace, I turned to the things that had once brought me joy. Music, books, long walks in nature. Yet, even these seemed to have lost their magic. The melodies that once uplifted now felt melancholic. The words on the pages blurred together, their stories failing to captivate. The tranquility of nature was overshadowed by the storm within.

I began to wonder if this was my new normal. If the person I had been was lost forever, replaced by this shadow of uncertainty and pain. It was a frightening thought, one that left me feeling even more isolated. I knew I needed to find a way through this, but the path was obscured, and I was unsure of where to begin.

In this state of emotional turmoil, I realized the importance of acknowledging the struggle. It was not a sign of weakness but a testament to the complexity of the human experience. Every tear shed, every moment of doubt, was a step towards understanding and ultimately healing. It was a slow process, filled with setbacks and small victories, but it was a journey worth undertaking.

SEEKING GUIDANCE

In the midst of adversity, I found myself grappling with questions that seemed to have no answers. The weight of uncertainty was suffocating, and I realized that I could not navigate this tumultuous path alone. The thought of reaching out for guidance was daunting, yet it became apparent that seeking wisdom from others was not a sign of weakness but a profound acknowledgment of my own humanity.

Reflecting on the moments that led me to this realization, I remember a conversation with an old friend. We hadn't spoken in years, but something compelled me to reconnect. Perhaps it was the familiarity of shared history or the comfort of knowing someone who had seen me through various stages of life. Our talk was raw and unfiltered, a mirror reflecting my inner turmoil and confusion. My friend's words were not solutions but rather gentle nudges, encouraging me to look within myself and find the strength I had forgotten existed.

Turning to books became another refuge. Pages filled with the wisdom of those who had walked similar paths became my silent mentors. I found solace in the stories of others who had faced their own adversities, their words resonating deeply within me. These authors, though distant in time and space, offered perspectives that illuminated my own struggles. It was in their reflections that I discovered new ways of thinking, new approaches to my own challenges.

There was also the unexpected guidance from strangers. A chance encounter with a kind-hearted stranger at a coffee shop led to a profound conversation about resilience. Their story, laden with heartbreak and triumph, echoed my own experiences. This serendipitous meeting reminded me that wisdom often comes from the most unexpected places and that every person we meet has the potential to teach us something invaluable.

Family, too, played an essential role. Their unwavering support and unconditional love provided a foundation upon which I could rebuild my strength. They listened without judgment, offering advice rooted in genuine concern. Their presence was a constant reminder that I was not alone in my struggle, that my battles were shared and that their belief in me was a powerful source of encouragement.

Therapy became another pivotal source of guidance. Speaking with a professional allowed me to untangle the web of emotions that had ensnared me. Through these sessions, I learned to confront my fears, to understand the underlying causes of my anxiety, and to develop strategies to cope with the pressures I faced. Therapy was not an immediate fix but a gradual process of self-discovery and healing.

Through these varied sources of guidance, I began to piece together a more comprehensive understanding of my situation. Each interaction, each piece of advice, each moment of introspection contributed to a mosaic of insights that guided me forward. The journey through adversity became less about finding definitive answers and more about embracing the wisdom that came from multiple perspectives.

In seeking guidance, I found a community of voices that collectively strengthened my resolve. The path was still fraught with challenges, but I was no longer navigating it in isolation. The wisdom and support of others became the compass that directed me toward a place of renewed hope and resilience.

MOMENTS OF DOUBT

As I ventured further into the labyrinth of my struggles, I encountered periods where the weight of uncertainty seemed almost unbearable. These moments were not mere fleeting thoughts but rather extended episodes that cast long shadows over my sense of purpose and direction. It was during these times that I questioned the very essence of my path. Was I truly capable of overcoming the hurdles that lay before me? Did I possess the fortitude to continue, or was I deluding myself with false hope?

One particularly vivid memory stands out, a night when sleep eluded me and my mind raced with doubts. The silence of the house amplified every anxious thought, turning them into a cacophony that drowned out any semblance of peace. I remember staring at the ceiling, feeling a profound sense of isolation. It was as if the walls of my room were closing in, mirroring the confines of my mind. The usual reassurances seemed hollow, and the familiar comforts offered no solace.

In these dark hours, I grappled with the notion of failure. The fear of not measuring up to my own expectations, let alone those of others, was paralyzing. It was not just the fear of falling short but the dread of what that failure represented—a confirmation of my deepest insecurities and a validation of every doubt that had ever crossed my mind. The thought of disappointing those who believed in me was a weight that pressed heavily on my chest.

Yet, amid this turmoil, there was a sliver of awareness that this too was part of the process. The very act of questioning, of confronting my fears head-on, was a testament to my resilience. It was a necessary step in understanding not just my limitations but also my potential. The doubts, as crippling as they felt, were not roadblocks but rather signposts, guiding me to a deeper understanding of myself.

Reflecting on these moments, I recognize that doubt is an inevitable companion on the path of growth. It is not a sign of weakness but a natural response to the unknown. The key lies in how one responds to it. For me, it was about finding the balance between acknowledging my fears and not allowing them to dictate my actions. It was a dance between vulnerability and strength, where each step required a conscious effort to maintain equilibrium.

In seeking to navigate these periods of uncertainty, I turned to various sources of strength. Conversations with trusted friends and mentors provided a different perspective, often illuminating aspects of my situation that I had overlooked. Their words were like beacons, offering light in the fog of my confusion. Additionally, moments of introspection and mindfulness allowed me to reconnect with my core values and motivations, serving as a reminder of why I had embarked on this journey in the first place.

These moments of doubt, while challenging, ultimately became catalysts for growth. They taught me the importance of patience, both with myself and with the process. They underscored the value of perseverance, not as a stubborn refusal to give up, but as a quiet, determined commitment to see things through, despite the uncertainties. And perhaps most importantly, they revealed that true strength lies not in the absence of doubt but in the courage to face it, to question it, and to continue moving forward regardless.

FINDING INNER STRENGTH

Reflecting upon the turbulent times that have shaped my path, I often find myself drawn to moments of quiet introspection. It's within these still moments that the concept of inner strength becomes not just a thought, but a palpable force. The trials I've faced have often felt like insurmountable walls, towering and unyielding. Yet, with each challenge, there was a whisper within, urging me to push forward, to dig deeper, and to find that well of resilience that lay hidden beneath layers of doubt and fear.

In the midst of adversity, it is easy to feel overwhelmed, to believe that our strength has abandoned us. But what I have come to realize is that strength is not always about grand gestures or heroic feats. Sometimes, it is about the quiet resolve to take one more step, to face another day, and to hold on to hope when everything around seems bleak. This inner fortitude is often forged in the fires of hardship, emerging stronger and more steadfast with each trial.

There have been times when I questioned my own capabilities, when the weight of the world seemed too heavy to bear. During these periods, I turned inward, seeking solace in reflection and meditation. It was in these quiet moments that I discovered the true essence of my inner strength. It is not a constant, unyielding force, but rather a dynamic, evolving presence that adapts and grows with each experience.

The journey to uncover this strength is deeply personal and unique to each individual. For me, it involved acknowledging my vulnerabilities and embracing them as part of my human experience. It required a shift in perspective, viewing challenges not as obstacles, but as opportunities for growth. This shift did not happen overnight; it was a gradual process, filled with setbacks and moments of doubt. But with each step, I felt a little stronger, a little more capable.

Support from loved ones played a crucial role in this process. Their unwavering belief in my abilities, even when I doubted myself, provided a foundation upon which I could build. They reminded me that strength is not about standing alone, but about leaning on others when needed. This interconnectedness, this web of support, is a testament to the power of human connection in fostering resilience.

Moreover, I found that engaging in activities that brought me joy and fulfillment helped to replenish my inner reserves. Whether it was through creative expression, physical exercise, or simply spending time in nature, these moments of joy acted as a counterbalance to the weight of adversity. They served as reminders that life, despite its challenges, is also filled with beauty and wonder.

Through these experiences, I have come to understand that inner strength is not a destination, but a continuous process of self-discovery and growth. It is about finding the courage to face our fears, the resilience to withstand life's storms, and the grace to accept ourselves, flaws and all. This strength is a testament to the human spirit's capacity to endure, to adapt, and to thrive, even in the face of the most daunting challenges.

As I continue to navigate the complexities of life, I hold onto the lessons learned during these times of adversity. They have shown me that inner strength is not a finite resource, but an ever-present force, ready to be called upon whenever needed. It is a reminder that within each of us lies a wellspring of resilience, waiting to be discovered and harnessed, guiding us through the darkest of times and into the light.

Chapter 6: A New Direction

REEVALUATING GOALS

The moments when life throws its hardest punches often become the crucible in which our true selves are forged. Struggle, pain, and adversity prompt us to look inward and question the paths we have chosen. It is during these times that the goals we once held dear may no longer seem relevant or meaningful. We come face-to-face with the need to reassess and reframe our aspirations, not as a sign of defeat, but as a testament to our growth.

In those quiet, reflective hours, we begin to ask ourselves the tough questions. What was the driving force behind our original goals? Were they shaped by our own desires, or were they imposed by societal expectations, familial pressures, or the quest for approval? The clarity that adversity brings can strip away the superficial layers, revealing the core of our true intentions.

This process of reevaluation often feels like peeling an onion, each layer revealing another until we reach the heart of what truly matters. It requires courage to confront the possibility that our previous ambitions may no longer align with our evolved selves. As we sift through the remnants of our past objectives, we might find that what once seemed like an immovable mountain is now just a distant hill.

The beauty of this introspective journey lies in the rediscovery of our authentic selves. The goals that emerge from this period of reflection are often more aligned with our values and passions. They are born out of a deeper understanding of what fulfills us, rather than what we think should fulfill us. This newfound clarity can be both liberating and empowering, providing a renewed sense of direction and purpose.

Adversity teaches us that flexibility is not a weakness, but a strength. The ability to pivot and adapt our goals in response to life's challenges is a testament to our resilience. It is not about abandoning our dreams but reshaping them to fit the new landscape of our lives. This adaptability ensures that our goals remain relevant and attainable, even in the face of unforeseen obstacles.

Moreover, reevaluating goals in the wake of adversity often fosters a sense of gratitude. The trials we endure can illuminate the preciousness of the present moment and the importance of cherishing small victories. This shift in perspective can transform our approach to goal-setting, emphasizing the process over the outcome, and the journey over the destination.

The act of reevaluation is not a solitary endeavor. Sharing our reflections with trusted friends, mentors, or counselors can provide valuable insights and perspectives. These conversations can serve as mirrors, reflecting back aspects of ourselves that we may have overlooked. They can also offer support and encouragement as we navigate this complex terrain.

Ultimately, the process of reevaluating our goals after facing adversity is a profound act of self-compassion. It acknowledges our growth, honors our experiences, and respects our evolving needs and desires. It is an affirmation that we are not static beings, but ever-changing, ever-growing individuals capable of redefining our paths as we continue to learn and evolve.

In this light, adversity becomes not just a challenge to overcome, but a catalyst for deeper understanding and more meaningful aspirations. It invites us to pause, reflect, and ultimately, to realign our goals with the truest version of ourselves.

EXPLORING OPPORTUNITIES

Adversity often feels like an insurmountable wall, a barrier that keeps us from the life we envision. But within every challenge lies a hidden opportunity, waiting to be discovered. Reflecting on my own experiences, I realize that the moments of greatest difficulty were also the moments ripe with potential for growth and transformation.

When I faced my most daunting obstacles, I initially saw them as setbacks, threats to my progress and well-being. It was only through introspection and a shift in perspective that I began to see them differently. I understood that adversity could be a catalyst for change, pushing me to explore paths I might never have considered otherwise. It was as if the universe was nudging me to look beyond my immediate discomfort and see the broader landscape of possibilities.

One pivotal experience stands out in my mind. I was at a crossroads, facing a professional failure that shattered my confidence. At first, I was consumed by self-doubt and regret, questioning my abilities and my worth. But as the days passed and the initial sting of disappointment faded, I started to view the situation through a different lens. This failure wasn't just a dead end; it was a chance to reevaluate my goals and priorities. It prompted me to ask myself what I truly wanted and what was genuinely fulfilling.

I began to see that the skills and knowledge I had acquired were not wasted but could be redirected towards new ventures. The setback became a springboard for innovation and creativity. I started to explore opportunities that aligned more closely with my passions and values, leading me to a career path that felt more authentic and rewarding.

In another instance, a personal loss left me feeling empty and lost. The grief was overwhelming, and for a time, it seemed like there was no way forward. But as I navigated through the pain, I found a profound sense of empathy and connection with others who had experienced similar losses. This shared understanding opened up new avenues for support and community. I discovered that by helping others through their struggles, I could also heal my own wounds. The adversity had given me a deeper sense of purpose and a way to transform my sorrow into something meaningful.

Reflecting on these experiences, I see that adversity is not just an obstacle to be overcome but a powerful teacher. It challenges us to look deeper, to find the hidden gems within our struggles. It encourages us to step out of our comfort zones and take risks that we might otherwise avoid. By doing so, we can uncover opportunities that lead to personal and professional growth.

The key lies in our willingness to remain open and curious, to question our assumptions and explore new possibilities. It's about finding the courage to turn inward and ask ourselves what we can learn from our hardships. Through this process, we can transform adversity into a source of strength and resilience, discovering opportunities that we might never have imagined.

In essence, adversity can be a doorway to new beginnings, if we allow ourselves to see it that way. It's a reminder that within every challenge lies the potential for growth, and that by exploring these opportunities, we can create a richer, more fulfilling life.

TAKING RISKS

The path of life is strewn with obstacles, uncertainties, and moments that demand a leap of faith. Reflecting on my own experiences, it becomes clear that taking risks has been an essential part of my journey through adversity. Each decision to step into the unknown has not only shaped my character but also provided invaluable lessons that have fortified my resilience.

One vivid memory stands out from my early career days. I was offered a position in a city far from home, a place where I had no friends or family. The comfort of familiarity tugged at me, urging me to stay within the confines of what I knew. Yet, there was a whisper of possibility, a chance to grow both professionally and personally. The decision to relocate was not easy; it was fraught with fears of isolation and failure. However, that choice became a cornerstone of my development, teaching me that the most profound growth often occurs outside of our comfort zones.

This experience taught me that risk-taking is not synonymous with recklessness. It is a calculated decision, a weighing of potential rewards against possible setbacks. In my case, the move led to new opportunities, enriching experiences, and a network of connections that I would have never encountered had I stayed put. The key was not just in making the leap but in preparing for it, understanding the stakes, and being ready to adapt to the outcomes.

Adversity often presents itself as a test, challenging us to step beyond our perceived limitations. There was a time when I faced a significant health scare, a diagnosis that threatened to upend my life. The easy path would have been to succumb to despair, to allow the fear to dictate my actions. Instead, I chose to confront it head-on, seeking out the best medical advice, adopting a healthier lifestyle, and surrounding myself with a support system. This proactive approach was a risk in itself, demanding a shift in mindset and habits. The result was a newfound appreciation for life and a deeper understanding of my own strength and resilience.

In professional settings, risk-taking can manifest in various forms— advocating for an innovative idea, challenging the status quo, or pursuing a project with uncertain outcomes. Each of these actions carries potential for failure, but they also hold the promise of significant rewards. I recall a particular instance when I proposed a radical change in our company's workflow. The suggestion was met with skepticism and resistance, yet I believed in its potential to streamline operations. The initial phase was rocky, with unforeseen challenges and pushback from colleagues. However, persistence and adaptability led to eventual success, transforming not just the workflow but also the organizational culture towards a more open and innovative mindset.

These experiences underscore the essence of taking risks: it is about confronting fear, making informed decisions, and being willing to face the consequences. It is not about the absence of fear but rather the recognition that fear can be a catalyst for action. Through each risk taken, I have learned that failure is not the end but a stepping stone towards greater achievements. It is in the willingness to take that leap, despite the uncertainty, that we often find our greatest strengths and most profound growth.

Reflecting on these moments, it is evident that the courage to take risks has been a pivotal element in navigating adversity. It has taught me that the unknown is not something to be feared but embraced as a realm of endless possibilities. Through risk-taking, I have discovered resilience, adaptability, and a deeper understanding of my own capabilities.

LEARNING FROM MISTAKES

Mistakes are often viewed through a lens of regret and disappointment. Yet, within each error lies a hidden opportunity for growth and self-discovery. This realization dawned on me during a particularly challenging period, when every misstep seemed to compound my sense of failure. It was during these moments of vulnerability that I began to understand the profound lessons embedded within my mistakes.

Reflecting on my past, I see how my initial reaction to errors was one of frustration and self-criticism. I would replay scenarios in my mind, dissecting every detail to pinpoint where I went wrong. This relentless self-examination, while exhausting, laid the foundation for a deeper understanding of my actions and their consequences. Over time, I learned that the true value of mistakes lies not in the error itself, but in the insights gained from it.

One pivotal mistake stands out vividly in my memory. I had taken on a project that was far beyond my expertise, driven by an eagerness to prove myself. Predictably, the project floundered, and I was left to face the repercussions. Initially, I was consumed by a sense of defeat. However, as the dust settled, I began to analyze what went wrong. I recognized my overestimation of my abilities and my lack of proper planning. This realization was a turning point. It taught me the importance of honest self-assessment and the necessity of seeking help when needed.

Mistakes also have a way of revealing our true character. In the face of failure, we are stripped of our pretenses and forced to confront our vulnerabilities. It is in these moments that resilience is forged. I recall a time when a miscommunication at work led to a significant setback for my team. Instead of assigning blame, we collectively took responsibility and worked towards a solution. This experience not only strengthened our teamwork but also highlighted the importance of accountability and collaboration.

Moreover, mistakes can serve as catalysts for innovation. When traditional methods fail, we are compelled to think creatively and explore alternative approaches. This was evident when a failed marketing campaign forced my team to re-evaluate our strategy. The failure pushed us to experiment with unconventional ideas, ultimately leading to a successful and innovative campaign. This taught me that setbacks can be a breeding ground for creativity and new perspectives.

In the grand tapestry of life, mistakes are the threads that add depth and texture. They remind us that perfection is an illusion and that growth is a continuous process. Each error, no matter how small, contributes to our evolving understanding of ourselves and the world around us. Embracing mistakes with humility and curiosity allows us to transform them into valuable lessons.

As I continue to navigate the complexities of life, I have come to appreciate the role of mistakes in shaping my journey. They are not merely obstacles to be avoided but integral components of a meaningful and fulfilling life. By learning from my mistakes, I am constantly evolving, becoming more resilient, and gaining a deeper appreciation for the intricate dance between success and failure.

BUILDING MOMENTUM

Life often feels like a series of uphill battles, each one steeper than the last. There are moments when it seems like all the effort is for naught, and the weight of adversity threatens to crush the spirit. But within those moments lies an opportunity to build something invaluable: momentum.

Reflecting on those tough times, it becomes clear that every small victory matters. Each step forward, no matter how insignificant it might seem, contributes to a larger picture. It's like pushing a boulder uphill; the initial effort is immense, but with each push, the boulder moves a little further, and the path becomes slightly more navigable. This is the essence of momentum in the face of adversity.

The journey starts with a single step, often taken in the dark, with no clear end in sight. That first step is the hardest, filled with doubt and fear. But once it's taken, the next one becomes just a bit easier. The key is to keep moving, even if progress is slow. Consistency, more than speed, is the true ally here. Each small action builds upon the last, creating a rhythm that gradually propels one forward.

Consider the times when giving up seemed like the only option. Those moments, when revisited, reveal a resilience that wasn't apparent at the time. Each decision to continue, despite the odds, added to an internal reservoir of strength. This reservoir isn't built overnight; it's a cumulative process, where every bit of effort contributes to a growing sense of capability and confidence.

Momentum also involves a shift in mindset. It's easy to view setbacks as failures, but they can also be seen as learning experiences. Each obstacle overcome is a testament to one's ability to adapt and persevere. This shift in perception transforms challenges into stepping stones rather than stumbling blocks. It's about recognizing that progress isn't always linear and that sometimes, the most significant growth happens during periods of struggle.

Support systems play a crucial role in maintaining momentum. Friends, family, mentors, and even brief encounters with strangers can provide the encouragement needed to keep going. Their belief in one's abilities often serves as a powerful counterbalance to self-doubt. Sharing the journey with others not only lightens the load but also provides different perspectives and insights that can spark new solutions and ideas.

Self-care is another vital component. It's impossible to maintain momentum without taking care of oneself. This means acknowledging the need for rest, nourishment, and mental well-being. Burnout is a real threat, and ignoring it can halt progress entirely. Taking time to recharge isn't a sign of weakness but a necessary step to ensure continued forward movement.

Looking back, it's evident that momentum isn't just about the physical act of moving forward; it's about cultivating a mindset that embraces persistence. It's about recognizing that every small effort counts and that over time, these efforts compound to create significant change. The path may be fraught with difficulties, but each challenge faced and overcome adds to the momentum that propels one towards their goals.

In this reflection, there's a profound realization that adversity, while daunting, is also an opportunity. It's an opportunity to build momentum, to grow stronger, and to move closer to becoming the person one aspires to be. Each step, each push, each moment of perseverance contributes to a powerful, unstoppable force that carries one forward.

Chapter 7: Support Systems

FAMILY BONDS

Family has always been the thread woven intricately through the fabric of my life, binding together moments of joy, sorrow, and everything in between. Each member of my family brings their own unique color to the tapestry, creating a rich and complex pattern that defines who I am. Reflecting on my experiences, it becomes clear that the bonds we share are not merely connections by blood, but by shared experiences, mutual support, and an unspoken understanding that transcends words.

Growing up, the family home was a sanctuary, a place where the outside world's chaos could be momentarily forgotten. Within those walls, I found solace in the presence of my family. My family, with their unwavering love and guidance, were the anchors that kept me steady even during the stormiest of times. They taught me resilience, showing me that adversity is not an end, but a beginning of growth and self-discovery.

My siblings, on the other hand, were my first friends, confidants, and occasional rivals. We navigated the labyrinth of childhood together, learning valuable lessons from each other along the way. The arguments, laughter, and shared secrets forged an unbreakable bond, one that has only grown stronger with time. Each of us has walked different paths, yet our journeys are forever intertwined by the memories and values instilled in us by our upbringing.

One of the most profound lessons I have learned from my family is the importance of empathy and compassion. Watching my parents extend a helping hand to those in need, even when they themselves were struggling, instilled in me a deep sense of humanity. They showed me that true strength lies not in avoiding adversity, but in facing it with an open heart and a willingness to support others.

There were times when life's challenges seemed insurmountable, and it was during these moments that the strength of our family bonds was truly tested. Illness, financial hardships, and personal losses could have easily torn us apart, but instead, they brought us closer. We leaned on each other, finding comfort and strength in our shared resilience. These experiences taught me that adversity, while painful, can also be a catalyst for deeper connections and personal growth.

As I reflect on my relationship with my family, I realize that these bonds have shaped my identity in profound ways. They have taught me the value of perseverance, the importance of kindness, and the power of unconditional love. These lessons have become the foundation upon which I build my life, guiding me through my own struggles and triumphs.

Even as we grow older and our lives take us in different directions, the bond we share remains a constant source of strength and inspiration. The memories we have created together serve as a reminder of where we come from and the values we hold dear. In the ever-changing landscape of life, my family is the unchanging North Star, guiding me through both calm waters and turbulent storms.

In the end, it is the family bonds that provide the strength to face life's adversities with courage and grace. They are the roots that ground us, the wings that lift us, and the heart that beats within us, reminding us that, no matter what challenges we face, we are never truly alone.

FRIENDS WHO STAYED

In the darkest moments, true friendships reveal their strength and depth. The trials I faced were not just personal battles; they became a litmus test for the relationships I held dear. Some connections, once thought unbreakable, faltered under the weight of adversity. Yet, amidst the retreat of many, there were those who stood steadfast, their loyalty unwavering.

Reflecting on those times, I realize that the friends who stayed did more than just offer a shoulder to cry on. They became my pillars, grounding me when everything else seemed to be in chaos. Their presence was not always about grand gestures or profound words. Often, it was the simple acts of kindness, the quiet understanding, and the unspoken support that made the most significant difference.

One such friend, Neha, comes to mind. Her ability to sense my turmoil without me uttering a word was uncanny. She would show up at my door with a warm meal, a comforting smile, and an open heart. Neha's empathy was a balm to my wounded spirit. She never tried to fix my problems or offer unsolicited advice. Instead, she listened, truly listened, and in doing so, she made me feel seen and heard.

There was also Vikas, whose humor became my refuge. In the bleakest of times, he could make me laugh, reminding me that joy could still be found, even in the smallest moments. Vikas's laughter was infectious, and his ability to find light in the darkest of places was a gift. He taught me that while it was essential to acknowledge pain, it was equally important to seek out moments of happiness.

Then there was Seema, whose resilience was a source of inspiration. She had faced her own share of challenges and emerged stronger. Seema's strength was not just in her ability to overcome but in her willingness to share her journey with me. She showed me that vulnerability was not a weakness but a testament to one's courage. Through her, I learned that it was okay to lean on others and that seeking support did not diminish my strength.

As I navigated through my struggles, these friends became my anchors. Their unwavering support was a testament to the power of genuine connection. They reminded me that I was not alone, that my worth was not defined by my hardships, and that I had the strength to persevere.

Looking back, the friends who stayed were not just companions; they were co-authors of my story. They helped me write chapters of resilience, hope, and renewal. Their presence was a constant reminder that even in the face of adversity, there is beauty in human connection. They taught me that true friendship is not about being there for the good times but about standing by each other through the storms.

In their steadfastness, I found the courage to face my challenges. Their unwavering belief in me became the foundation upon which I rebuilt my life. The friends who stayed did more than just offer support; they helped me rediscover my strength and reminded me that, even in the darkest moments, there is always a glimmer of light.

MENTORS AND GUIDES

In the labyrinth of life's challenges, certain individuals emerge who possess the uncanny ability to illuminate our path, offering wisdom and guidance when we need it most. Reflecting on my own experiences, I have come to understand the profound impact that mentors and guides have on our personal growth and resilience.

During times of adversity, these figures often appear almost serendipitously, their presence seeming to be orchestrated by some unseen hand. They may not always wear the mantle of a traditional mentor; sometimes, they are friends, colleagues, or even strangers who, through their words or actions, leave an indelible mark on our hearts and minds. Their influence often transcends the immediate context, becoming a beacon of hope and a source of strength.

There was a time in my life when I felt particularly adrift, navigating through a sea of uncertainty and self-doubt. It was then that I encountered an individual who would become a pivotal figure in my journey. This person did not offer grand solutions or miraculous cures for my troubles. Instead, they provided a listening ear, a compassionate heart, and a few simple yet profound insights that shifted my perspective. Their ability to see beyond the surface of my struggles, to recognize the potential within me that I had long forgotten, was nothing short of transformative.

The wisdom imparted by such mentors often comes in the form of subtle nudges rather than overt directives. They encourage us to explore our own depths, to question our assumptions, and to find our own answers. This process of self-discovery, guided by their gentle influence, becomes a powerful tool for overcoming adversity. These mentors do not seek to impose their will upon us; rather, they empower us to reclaim our own agency.

In reflecting on these relationships, I am reminded of the concept of "holding space." A true mentor is someone who can hold space for us, allowing us to express our fears, our hopes, and our dreams without judgment. This act of holding space creates a safe environment where we can confront our vulnerabilities and begin the healing process. It is in this space that we often find the clarity and courage needed to move forward.

The impact of mentors and guides extends far beyond the moments of crisis. Their teachings and the example they set become woven into the fabric of our lives, influencing our decisions and actions long after the initial encounter. They leave us with a legacy of resilience, a reminder that we are capable of navigating even the most tumultuous of waters.

Reflecting on the mentors in my own life, I am filled with a deep sense of gratitude. They have been the quiet architects of my resilience, helping to shape the person I have become. Their influence is a testament to the power of human connection and the profound difference one person can make in another's life.

In recognizing the significance of mentors and guides, we are also reminded of our own potential to be that source of light for others. Each of us, through our experiences and insights, has the ability to offer guidance and support to those who may be struggling. In doing so, we contribute to a cycle of resilience and empowerment that can ripple outwards, touching countless lives.

Thus, in the tapestry of adversity, mentors and guides are the threads of hope and wisdom that help us weave a narrative of strength and perseverance. Their presence is a gift, one that continues to inspire and uplift us as we navigate the complexities of life.

COMMUNITY CONNECTIONS

The small town where I grew up always seemed like a backdrop to my personal struggles. It wasn't until I began to truly observe the intricate web of relationships and support around me that I realized the power of community. The people, with their familiar faces and shared experiences, had a way of lifting the weight of adversity, even when they themselves were burdened by their own challenges.

One afternoon, as I walked through the town square, I noticed Mrs. Sharma, the elderly woman who owned the local bakery. She was a fixture in our community, known for her kindness and her delicious pastries. Despite her advanced age and the arthritis that gnawed at her hands, she never missed a day of work. Her resilience was a quiet testament to the strength that lay within us all.

On a particularly tough day, when my own troubles seemed insurmountable, I found myself at her bakery. The smell of freshly baked bread and the warmth of the space provided a temporary solace. Mrs. Sharma, with her gentle smile, handed me a warm bun and simply said, "You're not alone." Those words, simple yet profound, resonated deeply. It wasn't just the bread that nourished me; it was the unspoken understanding and the shared humanity.

The local community center was another beacon of hope. It was a place where people gathered not just for events, but to connect and support each other. During one of the toughest periods in my life, I joined a support group there. Initially, I was hesitant, unsure of what to expect or how much to share. But as I listened to others recount their stories of loss, pain, and eventual healing, I realized that we were all bound by a common thread. Each story was a mirror, reflecting bits of my own journey, and in that reflection, I found solace and strength.

One of the most poignant moments came during a town fundraiser. A devastating storm had swept through, leaving many families without homes. The entire community rallied together, organizing food drives, clothing donations, and temporary shelters. It was during this time that I saw the true essence of community. People who had little to give, gave anyway. There was a collective spirit of resilience and compassion that transcended individual hardships.

In the midst of the chaos, I met a young man named Kush (Name Changed). He had lost everything in the storm, yet he was at the forefront of the relief efforts, helping others rebuild their lives. His unwavering spirit was infectious. We spent countless hours together, organizing supplies and offering support to those in need. Through our shared efforts, a deep bond formed. Kush's story of perseverance and his positive outlook on life served as a powerful reminder that adversity, while challenging, could be a catalyst for growth and connection.

Reflecting on these experiences, it became clear that the community was not just a backdrop to my struggles but an integral part of my journey. The connections I made, the shared moments of vulnerability, and the collective strength of the people around me were instrumental in navigating my own challenges. The town, with its tapestry of stories, taught me that in the face of adversity, we find strength not only within ourselves but also in the bonds we form with others.

THE POWER OF SUPPORT

Reflecting on my own experiences, I am continuously reminded of the undeniable strength derived from support systems. It is often said that no one is an island, and my path through adversity has made this truth unmistakably clear. The presence of others, whether family, friends, or even strangers, has been instrumental in navigating the stormy seas of life's challenges.

I recall a particularly difficult period when I felt utterly overwhelmed. The weight of my struggles seemed insurmountable, and the isolation was suffocating. It was in these moments of despair that the support of others became a lifeline. A simple gesture, a listening ear, or a word of encouragement from those around me provided a sense of solace and hope. These acts, though seemingly small, had a profound impact on my ability to persevere.

Support is not merely about the physical presence of others; it encompasses emotional, mental, and sometimes even spiritual dimensions. Emotional support often came in the form of empathy and understanding. Friends who took the time to truly listen, without judgment, allowed me to express my fears and anxieties openly. This validation of my feelings was crucial in alleviating the burden of carrying them alone.

Mental support often arrived through shared wisdom and advice. I found that those who had faced similar adversities could offer perspectives and strategies that I had not considered. Their experiences became a source of inspiration and guidance, illuminating paths I had not seen. It was through these shared stories that I discovered the power of community and the collective strength it holds.

There is also a spiritual aspect to support that cannot be overlooked. For some, this may come from a higher power or a sense of connectedness to something greater than oneself. For me, it was the realization that we are all interconnected, and that the kindness and compassion we extend to others ultimately creates a web of support that can catch us when we fall. This interconnectedness fostered a sense of belonging and purpose, reinforcing the idea that we are never truly alone in our struggles.

Reflecting on these experiences, it becomes clear that support is a multifaceted and dynamic force. It evolves and adapts to our needs, sometimes manifesting in unexpected ways. A chance encounter with a stranger, a supportive message from an acquaintance, or the unwavering presence of a loved one can all serve as beacons of light in times of darkness.

As I continue to navigate the ups and downs of life, the importance of support remains ever-present. It is a reminder that while adversity may be inevitable, facing it does not have to be a solitary endeavor. The strength and resilience derived from the support of others are invaluable, and they underscore the profound impact we can have on each other's lives.

In reflection, the power of support is a testament to the human spirit's capacity for compassion and connection. It is a reminder that, even in our darkest hours, there is always a source of light to be found in the presence of others. Through support, we find the courage to face our challenges and the strength to overcome them, together.

Chapter 8: Self-Discovery

UNDERSTANDING MYSELF

In the quiet moments when the world seems to stand still, I often find myself lost in thought, reflecting on the path that has brought me to where I am today. Life, with all its unpredictable twists and turns, has a way of revealing truths about ourselves that we might otherwise overlook. It is through these moments of introspection that I have come to a deeper understanding of who I am, shaped by the adversities I have faced.

As a child, I was filled with dreams and aspirations, unaware of the challenges that lay ahead. I believed in the simplicity of cause and effect – that hard work would inevitably lead to success, and kindness would be met with kindness in return. However, life soon taught me that this was not always the case. Disappointments and setbacks became familiar companions, each one leaving a mark on my spirit.

It was during these difficult times that I began to question my own resilience. How much could I endure before I broke? What did it mean to be strong in the face of adversity? These questions haunted me, pushing me to look deeper within myself for answers. I realized that my strength was not merely a measure of how much I could withstand, but rather how I responded to the challenges that came my way.

Through this process of self-discovery, I began to see that adversity was not an enemy to be feared, but a teacher to be respected. Each hardship carried with it a lesson, an opportunity to grow and evolve. It was through facing my fears and confronting my insecurities that I discovered the depths of my own courage. I learned that true strength lies not in the absence of fear, but in the willingness to move forward despite it.

One particular experience stands out in my memory as a turning point in my understanding of myself. I had faced a significant personal loss, one that left me feeling hollow and directionless. In the depths of my grief, I found myself questioning my purpose and my place in the world. It was a dark period, but it was also a time of profound introspection. I began to see that my identity was not solely defined by my successes or failures, but by my ability to find meaning and purpose even in the midst of suffering.

This realization brought with it a sense of liberation. I no longer felt the need to measure myself against external standards or societal expectations. Instead, I focused on cultivating a sense of inner peace and authenticity. I embraced my imperfections and acknowledged that they were an integral part of my unique journey.

As I continued to navigate the complexities of life, I found solace in the knowledge that I had the power to shape my own narrative. The adversities I faced were not roadblocks, but stepping stones, guiding me toward a deeper understanding of myself and my place in the world.

Each challenge, no matter how daunting, became an opportunity to refine my character and strengthen my resolve.

In the end, my journey of self-discovery taught me that understanding oneself is an ongoing process, one that requires patience, compassion, and a willingness to embrace the unknown. It is through facing our adversities with an open heart and a resilient spirit that we uncover the true essence of who we are. And in that understanding, we find the strength to not only survive but to thrive.

STRENGTHS AND WEAKNESSES

Reflecting on my journey through adversity, I have come to recognize that the interplay between strengths and weaknesses is far more complex than I initially thought. My strengths have often been the pillars that supported me during turbulent times, while my weaknesses have been the shadows that taught me humility and resilience.

One of my most profound strengths is my ability to adapt. Life rarely unfolds as planned, and the capacity to pivot, adjust, and find new paths has been crucial. This adaptability has been a lifeline, allowing me to navigate unexpected challenges with a sense of purpose and determination. It's not just about surviving the storm, but learning to dance in the rain. Adaptability has enabled me to see opportunities where others see obstacles, to turn setbacks into stepping stones.

However, this strength has a flip side. My adaptability sometimes leads to a lack of commitment. In my eagerness to adjust, I've occasionally abandoned pursuits too quickly, mistaking temporary obstacles for insurmountable barriers. This tendency has cost me valuable opportunities and experiences. Recognizing this pattern has been vital in learning to balance flexibility with perseverance.

Another strength that has guided me is empathy. Understanding and sharing the feelings of others has fostered deep connections and provided a support network during my most challenging times. Empathy has been a bridge, connecting me to people who have offered wisdom, comfort, and new perspectives. It's a strength that has enriched my life, making the journey through adversity more bearable and meaningful.

Yet, empathy can also be a double-edged sword. There are moments when my empathetic nature has overwhelmed me, leading to emotional exhaustion. Absorbing the pain and struggles of others, while dealing with my own, has sometimes left me feeling drained and incapacitated. Learning to set boundaries has been essential in maintaining my emotional health and ensuring that my empathy remains a strength rather than a liability.

Determination is another cornerstone of my resilience. The unwavering resolve to keep going, even when the odds seem insurmountable, has been instrumental in overcoming adversity. This inner drive has pushed me to achieve goals that once seemed out of reach, providing a sense of accomplishment and growth.

However, determination can also morph into stubbornness. There have been times when my relentless pursuit of a goal has blinded me to alternative paths or solutions. This stubbornness has occasionally led me down difficult roads, causing unnecessary stress and frustration. Recognizing when to persist and when to pivot has been a critical lesson, helping me to harness my determination more effectively.

Self-reflection has revealed that my weaknesses are not merely flaws but opportunities for growth. They have highlighted areas where I need to develop and improve, offering valuable insights into my character and behavior. Each weakness, when acknowledged and addressed, has the potential to become a strength.

Navigating the delicate balance between strengths and weaknesses has been an ongoing process of self-discovery. It's a dynamic interplay that shapes how I confront and overcome adversity. By understanding and embracing both aspects of myself, I have found a deeper sense of resilience and a more profound appreciation for the complexities of my journey.

PERSONAL GROWTH

Life has a peculiar way of pushing us into the depths of challenges, often when we least expect it. It is in these moments of adversity that we are confronted with our true selves. The mirror held up by hardship reflects not just our strengths, but also our vulnerabilities, fears, and insecurities. I have come to understand that these experiences, though painful, are the crucibles in which personal growth is forged.

Navigating through turbulent times, I often felt a whirlwind of emotions—fear, anger, confusion, and sometimes even despair. But amid this chaos, there was also a quiet, persistent voice urging me to look deeper. It was as if the universe was whispering that the answers I sought were not outside, but within me. This realization was both daunting and liberating. It meant that I had to confront parts of myself that I had long ignored or suppressed. It required a level of honesty and introspection that was uncomfortable, yet necessary.

Reflecting on these moments, I began to see patterns. Each adversity was not just a random occurrence, but a lesson in disguise. There were times I felt like giving up, but it was precisely in those moments of surrender that I found a reservoir of strength I never knew existed. It became evident that personal growth was not about the absence of challenges, but about how we respond to them. The more I faced my fears and insecurities head-on, the more resilient I became.

One significant aspect of this growth was learning to be kind to myself. Society often equates success with perfection, leading us to be our harshest critics. I realized that true growth comes from accepting our imperfections and understanding that they are an integral part of who we are. This shift in perspective allowed me to extend grace to myself, to see mistakes as opportunities for learning rather than as failures. It was a transformative process, one that required patience and self-compassion.

Another crucial element was the power of perspective. Adversity has a way of narrowing our vision, making us focus on the immediate pain and struggle. However, stepping back and viewing the bigger picture can be incredibly enlightening. It taught me that every setback was a setup for a comeback. Each obstacle was an opportunity to develop new skills, to build character, and to gain insights that I could not have acquired otherwise. This shift in mindset turned adversity from an enemy into a teacher.

Moreover, the journey of personal growth is deeply intertwined with the relationships we cultivate. During my toughest times, I found solace in the support of friends and family. Their encouragement and understanding were invaluable. It also made me realize the importance of being vulnerable and open with others. Sharing my struggles not only lightened the burden but also deepened my connections with those around me. It was a reminder that we are never truly alone in our struggles.

In the end, personal growth is a continuous, evolving process. It is about becoming more attuned to our inner selves, embracing our imperfections, and learning to view challenges as stepping stones rather than stumbling blocks. Each experience, whether triumphant or trying, contributes to the tapestry of our lives, making us more resilient, compassionate, and wise. Through adversity, we discover the strength within, and in doing so, we not only grow but also find a deeper, more meaningful connection with ourselves and the world around us.

NEW SKILLS

Learning to navigate through hardship often brings unexpected opportunities for growth. Among these, acquiring new skills stands as a testament to resilience and adaptability. These skills, whether they are practical or emotional, become the tools that we carry forward, enhancing our ability to face future challenges with greater confidence and competence.

In the midst of adversity, the first step towards developing new skills often begins with a shift in mindset. It's about recognizing that every obstacle presents a chance to learn something new. This perspective transforms moments of struggle into valuable learning experiences. For instance, when faced with a difficult situation, one might develop problem-solving abilities that were previously untapped. The pressure to find solutions can lead to innovative thinking, fostering creativity and resourcefulness that remain beneficial long after the immediate issue has been resolved.

Another critical aspect is the development of emotional intelligence. Adversity often pushes us to confront our emotions head-on, leading to a deeper understanding of ourselves and others. This heightened awareness can improve our ability to manage stress, empathize with others, and communicate more effectively. These interpersonal skills are invaluable, not just for personal relationships, but also for professional environments where collaboration and understanding are key.

Additionally, adversity can compel us to acquire practical skills that we might not have considered otherwise. For example, someone who loses their job might learn new technical skills to adapt to a different industry. This adaptability is crucial in a rapidly changing world, where the ability to pivot and learn new competencies can significantly impact one's career trajectory. The process of learning itself becomes a skill, fostering a mindset that is open to continuous growth and improvement.

Moreover, adversity often necessitates a reevaluation of priorities and goals. This introspection can lead to the discovery of passions and interests that were previously overlooked. Pursuing these newfound interests can result in the acquisition of skills that bring both personal fulfillment and professional advancement. Whether it's learning a new language, picking up a musical instrument, or diving into a new field of study, these pursuits enrich our lives and broaden our horizons.

One of the most profound skills developed through adversity is resilience. This isn't just about bouncing back from setbacks, but about developing a robust inner strength that can withstand future challenges. Resilience involves a combination of mental toughness, optimism, and the ability to maintain perspective. It's about learning to see failures as temporary and surmountable, rather than as insurmountable obstacles. This mindset not only helps in overcoming current difficulties but also prepares us for future adversities.

Furthermore, the process of overcoming adversity often involves seeking support from others, which can enhance our social skills. Building a network of supportive relationships requires effective communication, empathy, and trust-building. These relationships can provide invaluable support during tough times and can be a source of strength and encouragement. The ability to cultivate and maintain such relationships is a skill that enriches our lives on multiple levels.

In essence, the skills developed through adversity are diverse and multifaceted. They encompass practical abilities, emotional intelligence, resilience, and social skills. Each of these contributes to our overall growth and equips us to handle future challenges with greater ease. While the process of acquiring these skills may be fraught with difficulty, the end result is a more capable, confident, and well-rounded individual.

EMBRACING CHANGE

Change has always been a constant companion in our lives, though often we resist its presence. We cling to the familiar, seeking comfort in the known, even when it no longer serves us. Reflecting on my own experiences, I realize that the most profound growth often springs from the fertile ground of change.

There was a time when I found myself at a crossroads, facing a significant shift that I neither anticipated nor desired. The initial reaction was a cocktail of fear and resistance. Yet, as days turned into weeks, and weeks into months, I began to perceive the subtle wisdom hidden within the upheaval. It was as if the universe was gently nudging me out of my complacency, urging me to explore new horizons.

The first step in navigating this uncharted territory was acceptance. It wasn't about giving up or resigning myself to fate, but rather acknowledging the reality of the situation. Acceptance allowed me to release the tight grip of control I had been holding onto. It was liberating, a breath of fresh air amid the stifling confines of my old ways.

With acceptance came the clarity to see opportunities previously obscured by my reluctance. I started to identify skills and strengths that had lain dormant, waiting for the right moment to surface. This period of transformation became a canvas on which I could paint new possibilities. Each brushstroke was a testament to resilience, adaptability, and the innate human capacity for renewal.

One of the most valuable lessons learned during this phase was the importance of perspective. Shifting my viewpoint from seeing change as a threat to viewing it as a catalyst for growth was pivotal. It required a conscious effort to reframe my thoughts, to catch myself in moments of doubt and gently steer my mind towards optimism. This mental shift didn't happen overnight, but with persistence, it became a natural part of my mindset.

Support from others also played a crucial role. Sharing my journey with friends, family, and mentors provided a network of encouragement and wisdom. Their insights often illuminated paths I hadn't considered, and their belief in my ability to adapt reinforced my own confidence. It was a reminder that while change is an individual experience, we don't have to face it in isolation.

As I navigated through this period, I also discovered the power of letting go. Holding onto the past, to what was comfortable and known, only served to weigh me down. By releasing old expectations, I made room for new experiences and growth. It was a process of shedding the old skin to reveal a more resilient self beneath.

Looking back, it's clear that change, though initially daunting, was a profound teacher. It taught me to be flexible, to trust in the unfolding of life, and to find strength in vulnerability. Each challenge encountered along the way was a stepping stone, guiding me towards a deeper understanding of myself and the world around me.

In the end, the journey through change was not just about surviving new circumstances but thriving within them. It was about finding the courage to step into the unknown with an open heart and mind, ready to learn and grow. This chapter of my life stands as a testament to the transformative power of change, a reminder that within every ending lies the seed of a new beginning.

Chapter 9: Overcoming Fear

IDENTIFYING FEARS

Looking inward often reveals the complexities of our fears, those shadows that loom large in the corridors of our minds. They are like silent specters, subtly influencing our actions, decisions, and even our dreams. Understanding these fears is akin to deciphering an intricate code, one that holds the potential to unlock a deeper understanding of oneself.

Reflecting on my personal experiences, I have come to realize that fears are not always rooted in the tangible world. They often stem from a place of vulnerability, a deep-seated sense of inadequacy or the dread of the unknown. This realization dawned on me during a particularly challenging phase of my life. The fear of failure seemed to overshadow every endeavor I undertook. It was as if an invisible hand was constantly holding me back, whispering doubts into my ear, making me question my worth and capabilities.

This fear was not born overnight. It was a culmination of past experiences, societal expectations, and internalized beliefs. Each misstep, each criticism, each disappointment added another layer to this formidable barrier. It wasn't until I started to peel back these layers, one by one, that I began to understand the root of my fears. It was a painful process, akin to opening old wounds, but it was also liberating.

One of the most profound realizations during this introspection was that fear is often a manifestation of our deepest desires. The fear of failure, for instance, is intrinsically linked to the desire for success and validation. By acknowledging this connection, I began to see my fears not as adversaries, but as indicators of what I truly valued. This shift in perspective was transformative. Instead of being paralyzed by my fears, I started to use them as a compass, guiding me towards my true aspirations.

Another critical insight was the recognition that fears are universal. Everyone, regardless of their background or achievements, harbors fears. This realization was both comforting and humbling. It reminded me of our shared humanity, the common threads that bind us all. By opening up about my fears, I found solace in the stories of others. Their experiences mirrored my own, and their resilience inspired me to confront my fears head-on.

The process of identifying fears also revealed the importance of self-compassion. It is easy to be harsh on oneself, to view fears as weaknesses or flaws. However, this mindset only serves to exacerbate the problem. By treating myself with kindness and understanding, I was able to create a safe space for introspection. This gentle approach allowed me to delve deeper into my psyche, to uncover fears that I had long buried.

In this reflective journey, I also discovered the power of mindfulness. By staying present and observing my thoughts without judgment, I was able to gain clarity. This practice helped me to distinguish between irrational fears and genuine concerns. It provided a sense of detachment, enabling me to view my fears objectively and address them constructively.

Identifying fears is not a one-time endeavor. It is an ongoing process, one that requires patience and persistence. Each new challenge brings with it a fresh set of fears, but with each confrontation, I grow stronger and more resilient. This continuous cycle of introspection and growth has become an integral part of my life, a testament to the transformative power of self-awareness.

Reflecting on this journey, I am reminded of the words of Carl Jung: "Who looks outside, dreams; who looks inside, awakes." By looking inward and identifying my fears, I have embarked on a path of self-discovery, one that has enriched my life in ways I could never have imagined.

FACING CHALLENGES

Adversity & Me is a book that delves deeply into the human experience of facing and overcoming challenges. As I reflect on the myriad obstacles that life has thrown my way, I realize that these moments of hardship have shaped me in ways I could never have anticipated.

When I think back on those tough times, it's not just the pain or the struggle that stands out, but also the unexpected lessons and strengths I discovered within myself. There were moments when the weight of the world felt unbearable, and giving up seemed like the easiest option. Yet, it was precisely in those moments of vulnerability that I found a wellspring of resilience.

One particular instance comes to mind. I was at a crossroads, grappling with both personal and professional setbacks. The sense of defeat was overwhelming, and it felt as though every effort I made was met with resistance. I remember sitting alone in my room, questioning my worth and capabilities. It was a dark place, one that many of us have visited at some point in our lives.

During this period of introspection, I realized that the challenge wasn't just the external circumstances but also my internal dialogue. The negative self-talk, the doubts, and the fears were my true adversaries. Recognizing this was the first step toward change. I began to understand that while I couldn't always control the external events, I could change how I responded to them.

This shift in perspective was transformative. Instead of viewing challenges as insurmountable obstacles, I started to see them as opportunities for growth. It wasn't an overnight change, and there were many setbacks along the way. However, each small victory built upon the last, creating a foundation of confidence and resilience.

Support from friends and family played a crucial role during this time. Their unwavering belief in me, even when I couldn't see the light at the end of the tunnel, provided the strength to keep going. It's a humbling experience to lean on others, to admit that you need help. But in doing so, I learned the value of community and connection.

Another key lesson was the importance of self-care. In the midst of adversity, it's easy to neglect one's well-being. I found solace in simple practices like journaling, meditation, and spending time in nature. These moments of peace and reflection allowed me to recharge and gain clarity. They became my sanctuary, a place where I could process my emotions and find a sense of balance.

Looking back, I see that each challenge was a test, not of my abilities, but of my spirit. They forced me to dig deep, to confront my fears, and to push beyond my perceived limits. In doing so, I discovered strengths I never knew I had and developed a deeper understanding of myself.

The road was far from easy, and there were times when I stumbled and fell. But each fall taught me something valuable, and each rise made me stronger. Adversity, I realized, was not my enemy but my greatest teacher. It showed me that within every struggle lies the seed of opportunity, and within every setback, the potential for a comeback.

BUILDING COURAGE

Courage isn't something that one can simply acquire overnight. It is a quality that develops gradually, often through the trials and tribulations we face in life. When I reflect on my own experiences, I see a mosaic of moments—some painful, others enlightening—that have collectively contributed to building my courage. Each instance, no matter how small or seemingly insignificant, has played a crucial role in shaping my inner strength.

One of the earliest memories that comes to mind is from my childhood. I was a timid child, often afraid to speak up or stand out. The schoolyard was a battleground, and I was an unwilling participant. It wasn't until a particular incident, where I was pushed to the edge of my comfort zone, that I began to understand the essence of courage. A friend was being bullied, and though my heart pounded with fear, something inside me compelled me to step in. That act, though small, was monumental for me. It was the first time I realized that courage isn't the absence of fear, but the decision to act despite it.

As I grew older, the challenges became more complex. Adolescence brought its own set of trials, from academic pressures to social dynamics. Each challenge required a different kind of courage— sometimes it was the courage to admit I didn't know something, other times it was the courage to stand by my values when they were tested. The most significant lesson during these years was understanding that courage often involves vulnerability. Admitting weakness or asking for help can be incredibly daunting, but it is in these moments of vulnerability that true courage is forged.

In adulthood, the stakes became higher. Career choices, relationships, and personal aspirations demanded a level of courage I hadn't anticipated. I vividly recall the period when I decided to leave a stable job to pursue my passion. The fear of the unknown was paralyzing, but the greater fear of living a life unfulfilled pushed me forward. It was during this time that I learned the importance of self-belief. Courage, I discovered, often stems from an unwavering belief in oneself, even when the path ahead is unclear.

Life has a way of presenting us with situations that test our resolve. The loss of a loved one, for instance, is a profound test of courage. Grief can be overwhelming, and finding the strength to move forward requires immense inner fortitude. During such times, I found that courage often lies in the small, everyday acts of resilience—getting out of bed, facing the day, and allowing oneself to heal gradually.

Reflecting on these experiences, it becomes clear that courage is not a static trait but a dynamic one. It grows and evolves with each challenge faced and overcome. It is built through a series of choices—each one a testament to our ability to confront fear and uncertainty. The journey of building courage is ongoing, a continuous process of learning and growing.

In the tapestry of life, courage is the thread that holds everything together. It is what enables us to face adversity with grace and determination. As I continue to navigate the complexities of life, I am reminded that building courage is a lifelong endeavor, one that requires patience, reflection, and unwavering resolve.

SMALL VICTORIES

There are moments in life when the weight of challenges seems almost unbearable. Yet, within these struggles, there are glimmers of hope, small victories that serve as reminders of our resilience and strength. These seemingly minor triumphs often hold profound significance, shaping our path forward in ways we might not immediately recognize.

Reflecting on these small victories can be a deeply personal and transformative experience. They might not always be grand or celebrated by others, but their impact on our personal growth is undeniable. Each one represents a step forward, however small, in our journey through adversity.

Consider the first time you managed to get out of bed after days, weeks, or even months of feeling immobilized by depression. That moment, though it might seem insignificant to an outsider, is a testament to your inner strength and determination. It is a victory worth acknowledging and celebrating, for it signifies the beginning of a slow but steady climb out of the darkness.

Similarly, think about the times when you have faced overwhelming anxiety but still managed to push through and complete a task or attend an event. The courage it takes to confront and navigate these feelings is immense, and each instance is a small victory that builds upon the last, gradually fortifying your resilience.

These small victories are not just about overcoming emotional or mental hurdles. They can also be found in the physical realm. Perhaps you are recovering from an illness or injury, and each day brings a tiny improvement in your condition. The first time you can walk unaided, the first time you can lift a weight you once couldn't, or the first time you can sleep through the night without pain—all these moments are victories that mark progress and healing.

In the face of adversity, it is easy to overlook these small victories, especially when we are conditioned to value grand achievements and milestones. However, it is these incremental steps that often lay the foundation for larger successes. They teach us patience, perseverance, and the importance of self-compassion.

Reflecting on these moments can also shift our perspective, helping us to see the positive amidst the challenges. It allows us to recognize our own growth and appreciate the effort we have put into overcoming obstacles. This shift in perspective can be empowering, reminding us that we are capable of more than we often give ourselves credit for.

It is important to take the time to acknowledge and celebrate these small victories. Whether it is through journaling, sharing with a trusted friend, or simply taking a moment to reflect quietly, recognizing these achievements reinforces our progress and motivates us to continue moving forward.

The journey through adversity is rarely straightforward, but it is punctuated with these small victories that illuminate the path. They are the beacons of hope that guide us, reminding us that even in our darkest moments, we are capable of overcoming and growing stronger. Each small victory is a testament to our resilience, a reminder that we are moving forward, one step at a time.

TRANSFORMING FEAR INTO STRENGTH

Fear often grips us in ways that are both subtle and overwhelming. It lurks in the shadows of our mind, whispering doubts and magnifying insecurities. Yet, within the murky depths of fear lies a potent seed of strength waiting to be unearthed. Reflecting on my own experiences, I've come to understand that fear, rather than being an insurmountable obstacle, can be a powerful catalyst for personal growth.

The first step in transforming fear into strength is acknowledgment. Denying or suppressing fear only allows it to fester, growing more formidable with time. By facing it head-on, we begin to demystify its power. I recall a time when the fear of failure paralyzed me. It was during a crucial phase in my career when the stakes were high, and the margin for error seemed nonexistent. Instead of succumbing to the paralyzing grip of fear, I chose to confront it. This act of acknowledgment didn't eliminate the fear, but it did diminish its hold on me.

Understanding the root of fear is equally essential. Often, fear stems from past experiences, societal pressures, or internalized beliefs. Delving into these origins provides clarity and insight. For me, the fear of failure traced back to childhood moments where perfection was expected, and mistakes were met with criticism. This realization was liberating. It allowed me to reframe my perspective, viewing failures not as endpoints but as opportunities for learning and growth.

Transforming fear involves a conscious decision to step out of comfort zones. Comfort zones, while safe, are also limiting. They create an illusion of security that stifles growth and potential. I remember the first time I decided to speak publicly about my experiences. The fear was palpable, but so was the desire to grow. By stepping onto that stage, I not only conquered a personal fear but also discovered a newfound confidence. Each step outside the comfort zone, no matter how small, builds resilience and fortitude.

Support systems play a crucial role in this transformation. Sharing fears with trusted friends, mentors, or counselors can provide fresh perspectives and invaluable encouragement. During my most challenging times, the support of loved ones acted as a beacon of hope. Their belief in my abilities, even when I doubted myself, fortified my resolve. The act of voicing fears often diminishes their power, making them more manageable.

Mindfulness and self-compassion are indispensable tools in this journey. Fear often thrives on negative self-talk and harsh self-judgment. By cultivating mindfulness, we learn to observe our fears without being consumed by them. Self-compassion, on the other hand, teaches us to treat ourselves with the same kindness and understanding we would offer a friend. These practices create a mental space where fear can be transformed into a source of strength.

Reflecting on these strategies, it becomes evident that fear, when approached with the right mindset, can be a powerful ally. It challenges us, pushing us to explore uncharted territories within ourselves. Each encounter with fear, when met with courage and resilience, strengthens our inner core. The journey of transforming fear into strength is continuous, marked by moments of introspection, growth, and unwavering determination. Through this process, we discover that fear, rather than being a foe, can be a formidable teacher, guiding us towards our truest potential.

Chapter 10: Redefining Success

WHAT SUCCESS MEANS

Success is a concept that has intrigued, puzzled, and driven humanity for generations. It's a term that holds different meanings for different people, shaped by personal experiences, societal norms, and individual aspirations. For some, success is synonymous with wealth and material possessions; for others, it's about achieving personal happiness or making a meaningful impact on the world. Reflecting on what success means to me, especially through the lens of adversity, reveals layers of understanding that go beyond conventional definitions.

In the quiet moments of introspection, I find that success is less about the accolades and more about the journey of overcoming obstacles. Adversity has a way of stripping away the superficial layers, exposing the core of what truly matters. It's in the struggles, the setbacks, and the moments of doubt that we discover our resilience, strength, and capacity for growth. These experiences teach us that success is not a static destination but an evolving process.

Consider the times when life's challenges seemed insurmountable. The moments when the weight of the world pressed heavily on my shoulders, and the path forward was shrouded in uncertainty. It's in these moments that I learned the most about myself. Each hurdle became an opportunity for reflection, a chance to reassess my goals and priorities. Success, then, became about the ability to adapt, to find new ways forward even when the road ahead seemed blocked.

Looking back, I realize that the traditional markers of success—titles, awards, financial stability—while important, are not the sole indicators of a fulfilling life. The relationships we build, the kindness we extend, and the courage we muster in the face of adversity are equally, if not more, significant. These elements form the foundation of a life well-lived, a life where success is measured not just by external achievements but by inner growth and contentment.

The stories of those who have faced tremendous hardships and emerged stronger resonate deeply. Their narratives remind us that success is often born out of struggle. It's about finding the strength to rise after a fall, the determination to keep moving forward despite the odds. These individuals exemplify the idea that true success lies in the perseverance and resilience that adversity cultivates.

As I navigate through my own challenges, I find solace in the understanding that success is a deeply personal journey. It's about setting my own benchmarks and celebrating the small victories along the way. It's about recognizing that every setback is a setup for a comeback, and every failure is a lesson in disguise. This perspective allows me to appreciate the process, to find joy in the little things, and to stay grounded in the face of life's unpredictability.

In essence, success is a tapestry woven with threads of perseverance, resilience, and personal growth. It's about the ability to find meaning and purpose in the midst of adversity, to transform challenges into opportunities for self-discovery and improvement. As I continue to reflect on what success means to me, I am reminded that it's not just about where I end up, but how I get there and who I become along the way.

SETTING NEW GOALS

Reflecting on my path through adversity, I realized that my initial goals were born from a place of necessity, survival even. They were the stepping stones that carried me through the storm, but as the clouds began to part, I understood that the purpose of these goals had evolved. It was time to reassess and redefine what I aimed to achieve, not just to survive, but to thrive.

The first step in this process was introspection. I needed to understand what truly mattered to me now, in this new phase of my life. My previous goals were about getting back to a baseline of normalcy, but now I had the opportunity to aim higher. I asked myself what I was passionate about, what brought me joy, and what kind of legacy I wanted to leave behind. These questions were daunting, yet liberating.

It was crucial to set goals that were not only ambitious but also aligned with my core values. I found that when my goals resonated with my deepest beliefs, they became more than just targets; they became a source of motivation and inspiration. This alignment also made the journey toward achieving these goals feel more natural and less forced.

One of the key lessons I learned during this period was the importance of flexibility. Life is unpredictable, and clinging rigidly to a plan can lead to frustration and disappointment. By allowing myself the grace to adapt my goals as circumstances changed, I maintained a sense of progress and purpose. This flexibility did not mean abandoning my aspirations at the first sign of difficulty, but rather adjusting my approach and timelines as needed.

Another important aspect was setting both short-term and long-term goals. The long-term goals provided a vision of where I wanted to be, a destination to strive toward. However, the short-term goals were equally important as they offered immediate milestones to celebrate along the way. These smaller achievements kept my spirits high and reinforced the belief that I was on the right path.

Accountability also played a significant role in this process. Sharing my goals with trusted friends, family, or mentors provided a support system that encouraged me to stay committed. Their perspectives often offered valuable insights and helped me stay grounded. Moreover, discussing my goals openly created a sense of responsibility; knowing that others were aware of my aspirations motivated me to work diligently toward them.

As I set these new goals, I remained mindful of the balance between ambition and self-care. It was easy to get caught up in the excitement of new possibilities and push myself too hard. However, I had learned the hard way that burnout could be just as detrimental as inactivity. By pacing myself and incorporating periods of rest and reflection, I ensured that my pursuit of new goals was sustainable.

Throughout this transformative process, I discovered that setting new goals was not merely about achieving specific outcomes. It was about personal growth, resilience, and the continuous journey of self-discovery. Each goal I set and worked toward became a testament to my ability to overcome adversity and build a life that was not defined by past struggles but enriched by the lessons learned from them.

ACHIEVING BALANCE

The scales of life rarely rest perfectly balanced. One side might dip under the weight of professional demands, while the other rises with the lightness of personal joys. This precarious dance between extremes often leaves us teetering, searching for a middle ground where we can stand firm. Reflecting on my own experiences, I've come to realize that balance isn't a static state but a dynamic process—constantly shifting, recalibrating, and adapting to the ebb and flow of life's challenges and rewards.

My early years were marked by a relentless pursuit of academic excellence. The drive to outshine my peers and meet my parents' high expectations consumed me. Late nights spent poring over textbooks and early mornings filled with extracurricular activities left little room for anything else. I believed that sacrificing personal time was the price of success. It wasn't until I found myself physically and emotionally drained that I began to question this one-sided approach.

The turning point came during a particularly grueling semester. I was overwhelmed, juggling multiple responsibilities, and felt as though I was constantly falling short. A mentor noticed my struggle and offered a piece of advice that has since resonated deeply: "Life is like riding a bicycle. To keep your balance, you must keep moving." This simple analogy opened my eyes to the importance of momentum and adaptability.

Incorporating balance into my life required intentional changes. I started by setting boundaries, learning to say no to commitments that overextended me. It was a difficult shift, as I feared disappointing others and missing out on opportunities. However, I soon discovered that by prioritizing my well-being, I was able to show up more fully and effectively in all areas of my life.

Mindfulness practices became a cornerstone of my journey towards balance. Through meditation and reflective journaling, I began to understand the patterns of my thoughts and emotions. These practices offered a sanctuary amidst the chaos, allowing me to center myself and approach challenges with a clearer mind. The act of pausing, even briefly, provided a much-needed respite and a chance to recalibrate.

Physical activity also played a significant role in restoring balance. Regular exercise became not just a tool for physical health but a mental and emotional release. Whether it was a brisk walk in nature or an intense workout session, the movement helped to dissipate the stress and refocus my energy. It was during these moments that I often found clarity and inspiration, solutions to problems that had seemed insurmountable.

One of the most profound lessons was learning to seek and accept support. For a long time, I equated asking for help with weakness. However, opening up to friends, family, and colleagues revealed a network of strength and solidarity. Their perspectives and encouragement provided new insights and reminded me that I wasn't alone in my struggles.

Balancing the demands of life continues to be an ongoing practice, one that requires constant attention and adjustment. There are days when the scales tip too far in one direction, but I've learned to recognize the signs and take corrective measures. This dynamic equilibrium is a testament to resilience and self-awareness, a reminder that balance is not a destination but a continuous journey of growth and adaptation.

In reflecting on my path, it's clear that achieving balance is less about perfection and more about harmony. It's about finding a rhythm that allows us to navigate life's complexities with grace and intention. Through this lens, adversity becomes not an obstacle but a catalyst for deeper understanding and more profound balance.

CELEBRATING MILESTONES

Reflecting on the path we've walked, it's often the milestones, both big and small, that give us the strength to continue. These markers of progress are not just moments of achievement; they are the beacons that light our way through the dense fog of adversity. They remind us of our resilience and our ability to overcome, no matter how insurmountable the odds may seem.

When faced with life's challenges, it's easy to become consumed by the difficulties. Each obstacle can feel like a towering mountain, blocking our view of the horizon. However, every step forward, no matter how small, is a testament to our determination and willpower. It's important to pause and acknowledge these steps, to give ourselves credit for the progress we've made. This act of recognition is not about boasting but about affirming our capabilities and fortifying our resolve.

The first milestone often comes with the initial decision to confront adversity head-on. This decision, though it may seem insignificant at the moment, is the foundation upon which all future successes are built. It's a declaration of intent, a promise to ourselves that we will not be defeated. This moment deserves to be celebrated, for it marks the beginning of our transformation.

As we move forward, other milestones appear, sometimes in the most unexpected forms. They can be as subtle as a change in perspective or as tangible as a goal achieved. The first time we find ourselves smiling after a period of sorrow, the moment we realize we've gained strength from our struggles, or the instance when we help someone else because of the lessons we've learned—these are all milestones worth celebrating. They signify growth, healing, and the gradual reclaiming of our lives.

In the midst of adversity, it's crucial to create a space for these celebrations. They serve as reminders that we are progressing, even when progress feels slow. They help to shift our focus from what we have yet to achieve to what we have already accomplished. This shift in focus can be incredibly empowering, providing the motivation needed to continue moving forward.

The act of celebrating can take many forms. It might be a quiet moment of reflection, a journal entry, or sharing our achievements with a trusted friend. It could be treating ourselves to something special, or simply taking a moment to breathe deeply and appreciate how far we've come. The form of celebration is less important than the acknowledgment itself.

These milestones also serve another purpose: they build a roadmap of our resilience. Looking back on them, we can trace the path we've taken, seeing clearly the progress we've made. This retrospective view can be a powerful tool in moments of doubt, reminding us of our strength and our ability to persevere.

As we continue to navigate through life's challenges, let's remember to honor these milestones. They are not just markers of what we've achieved but symbols of our enduring spirit. Celebrating them is an act of self-love, a way to nurture our inner strength and maintain the momentum needed to continue overcoming the obstacles that lie ahead.

In the end, these milestones are the threads that weave the fabric of our journey through adversity, creating a tapestry that tells the story of our resilience, growth, and unwavering determination. They are the proof that we are capable of not just surviving but thriving, even in the face of life's greatest challenges.

A NEW PERSPECTIVE

Life has a way of presenting challenges that, at first glance, seem insurmountable. The weight of adversity can feel like an anchor, pulling us down into the depths of despair. Yet, it is within these very depths that we often find the most profound insights and growth. The crucible of hardship has a transformative power, reshaping our perspectives in ways we could never have imagined.

When faced with difficult times, the initial reaction is often one of resistance. We struggle against the tide, trying to maintain a semblance of control. However, it is in the act of letting go, of surrendering to the flow of life's unpredictable currents, that we begin to see things differently. This shift in mindset is not about giving up but about opening oneself up to new possibilities and understanding.

Reflecting on my own experiences, I recall moments where adversity seemed to engulf me completely. During these times, my vision was narrow, focused solely on the immediate pain and discomfort. But as the days turned into weeks and the weeks into months, a subtle change began to take place. The challenges that once seemed like insurmountable obstacles started to appear as opportunities for growth and learning. This wasn't a sudden epiphany but a gradual awakening to a new way of seeing the world.

One of the most significant lessons learned through adversity is the importance of perspective. When we are in the midst of a storm, it is easy to become consumed by the chaos around us. However, taking a step back, even if only for a moment, allows us to gain a clearer view of the bigger picture. This broader perspective can reveal patterns and connections that were previously hidden, offering insights that can guide us through the turmoil.

Adversity also teaches us about resilience. It shows us that we are capable of enduring far more than we ever thought possible. Each setback, each failure, each moment of pain, contributes to our inner strength. This resilience is not just about bouncing back but about moving forward with a deeper understanding and appreciation of our own capabilities.

Moreover, facing challenges head-on can lead to a greater sense of empathy and compassion. When we have personally experienced hardship, we become more attuned to the struggles of others. This heightened sensitivity fosters a sense of connection and community, reminding us that we are not alone in our journey. Shared experiences of adversity can forge bonds that are both deep and enduring.

It is also worth noting that adversity often sparks creativity and innovation. When traditional solutions fail, we are forced to think outside the box, to approach problems from new angles. This creative problem-solving can lead to breakthroughs that would never have been possible in more comfortable circumstances. Adversity, in this sense, becomes a catalyst for growth and progress.

In essence, the trials we face shape us in ways that are both subtle and profound. They challenge our preconceptions, push us beyond our limits, and ultimately lead us to a deeper understanding of ourselves and the world around us. While the journey through adversity is never easy, it is through this journey that we discover our true potential and gain a new perspective on life.

Chapter 11: The Road to Recovery

STARTING OVER

There I was, standing at the precipice of a new beginning, feeling the weight of my past experiences bearing down on me. The journey to this point had been fraught with challenges, each one a lesson in resilience and self-discovery. As I gazed into the uncertain future, I couldn't help but reflect on the moments that had brought me here, moments that had tested my strength and shaped my character.

The past had been a turbulent sea, with waves of adversity crashing against the fragile vessel of my life. Each wave, though daunting, had taught me to navigate the storm with a newfound sense of purpose. It was in the midst of these trials that I discovered the depth of my inner strength, a reservoir I had not known existed. The process of rebuilding, of picking up the shattered pieces and forging something new, had become a testament to my resilience.

There were days when the darkness seemed impenetrable, when the weight of my struggles threatened to pull me under. Yet, it was in these moments of despair that I found the flicker of hope, a beacon guiding me towards a brighter horizon. The support of loved ones, the wisdom gleaned from past mistakes, and the unwavering belief in my own potential became the lifelines that kept me afloat.

As I stood on the threshold of this new chapter, I was acutely aware of the scars that marked my journey. Each one told a story of survival, of battles fought and won. They were reminders of the strength that lay within me, a strength that had been forged in the crucible of adversity. These scars were not a source of shame, but rather a testament to my resilience and growth.

The process of starting anew was not without its challenges. There were moments of doubt, of fear that history might repeat itself. Yet, with each step forward, I felt a renewed sense of determination. The lessons of the past had equipped me with the tools to face whatever lay ahead. I had learned to trust in my ability to adapt, to find solutions where none seemed possible, and to persevere in the face of uncertainty.

This new beginning was an opportunity to redefine myself, to shed the limitations imposed by past failures and embrace the potential for growth and transformation. It was a chance to rewrite my story, to choose a path that aligned with my values and aspirations. The road ahead was uncharted, but it was also filled with promise and possibility.

In reflecting on the journey to this point, I realized that adversity had been both my greatest challenge and my greatest teacher. It had taught me the importance of resilience, the value of perseverance, and the power of hope. It had shown me that even in the darkest of times, there is always a way forward.

As I took the first steps into this new chapter, I carried with me the lessons of the past and the strength of my experiences. The future was uncertain, but I was ready to face it with courage and determination.

This was not just a new beginning; it was a testament to the resilience of the human spirit and the endless possibilities that lie ahead.

REBUILDING FINANCES

Looking back, the financial turmoil felt like an unending storm, each wave threatening to capsize any semblance of stability. The initial shock of financial loss was paralyzing. It was as though every security I had meticulously built over the years had crumbled in an instant. The nights were the hardest, filled with a cacophony of what-ifs and hows, as if my mind was perpetually caught in a loop of despair.

Yet, in those darkest moments, a tiny spark of resilience began to flicker. It was not immediate, nor was it always strong, but it persisted. I started by assessing the damage, combing through bank statements and bills, each number a stark reminder of the situation's gravity. It was a daunting task, but essential. Understanding the full scope of the problem was the first step towards any meaningful solution.

With a clearer picture, the next move was to create a plan. This was not just about numbers on a spreadsheet, but about reestablishing trust in my ability to manage and rebuild. I sought advice from financial advisors, read countless articles, and even attended workshops. Knowledge became my ally, a beacon guiding me through the fog of uncertainty.

Cutting unnecessary expenses was a painful but crucial step. It required a level of honesty with myself that was often uncomfortable. The things I thought I needed were stripped away, revealing what was truly essential. This process was not just about financial austerity, but also about redefining priorities and values. It was an exercise in humility and gratitude, finding contentment in simplicity.

In parallel, increasing income streams became a priority. This meant taking on additional work, exploring freelance opportunities, and even selling items that no longer served a purpose. It was exhausting, but each small success brought a renewed sense of purpose and control. The extra hours and effort were investments in a more stable future, and with each passing month, the fruits of these labors began to show.

Support from friends and family was invaluable. Their encouragement provided a lifeline, reminding me that I was not alone in this struggle. They offered more than just moral support; practical advice, shared experiences, and sometimes a helping hand when things seemed too overwhelming. This collective effort reinforced the importance of community and the strength that comes from leaning on others.

As the months turned into years, the financial landscape began to shift. The debts that once seemed insurmountable were gradually paid down, savings slowly rebuilt, and investments cautiously made. Each milestone, no matter how small, was a victory worth celebrating. It was not just about restoring what was lost, but about building something more resilient and sustainable.

Reflecting on this period, it is clear that rebuilding finances was as much an emotional and psychological journey as it was a financial one. The lessons learned extended far beyond dollars and cents. They were about perseverance, adaptability, and the unwavering belief in one's ability to overcome adversity. The path was neither easy nor quick, but it was transformative, reshaping not just my financial situation, but my entire approach to life's challenges.

This chapter of adversity revealed an inner strength that might have remained dormant without such trials. It taught the value of patience, the importance of strategic planning, and the power of community. Most importantly, it reaffirmed that even in the face of overwhelming odds, rebuilding is possible, and through that process, one can emerge stronger and wiser.

REESTABLISHING CAREER

The morning sunlight filtered through the blinds, casting a warm glow on the room where I sat with a cup of tea. It was one of those rare moments of tranquility, a brief respite from the chaos that had enveloped my life over the past few year. The road to recovery had been arduous, filled with countless setbacks and moments of self-doubt. But as I sipped my tea, I felt a newfound sense of determination. It was time to rebuild, to reestablish my career, and to reclaim the sense of purpose that had once driven me.

The first step was to take stock of my skills and experiences. I had spent years honing my craft, developing a unique set of abilities that had once made me a sought-after professional. But the landscape had changed, and so had I. The adversity I had faced had reshaped my perspective, teaching me lessons that no textbook or training program ever could. It was time to leverage these lessons and apply them in new and innovative ways.

Networking became my lifeline. Reaching out to former colleagues, mentors, and even acquaintances from industry events, I began to weave a web of connections that would prove invaluable. These conversations were more than just professional exchanges; they were opportunities to gain insights, to learn about emerging trends, and to discover potential opportunities. Each interaction rekindled a spark of hope, reminding me that I was not alone in this journey.

Updating my resume was more than just a formality; it was an exercise in self-reflection. As I listed my accomplishments and experiences, I was reminded of the resilience and tenacity that had carried me through the darkest times. The gaps in my employment history, once a source of shame, were now badges of honor that spoke to my ability to overcome adversity. Crafting a narrative that highlighted these strengths was empowering, transforming my resume from a mere document into a testament to my journey.

Continuing education became a priority. Enrolling in online courses and attending workshops, I sought to bridge the gap between my existing knowledge and the evolving demands of the industry. These learning opportunities not only enhanced my skill set but also reignited my passion for the field. With each new certification and completed course, my confidence grew, reinforcing my belief that I was ready to reenter the professional arena.

The job search itself was a test of patience and perseverance. Rejections and unresponsive employers were disheartening, but each setback only fueled my resolve. I tailored my applications, crafting personalized cover letters that spoke to my unique experiences and the value I could bring to potential employers. Interviews became opportunities to share my story, to demonstrate how adversity had shaped me into a more resilient and adaptable professional.

And then, finally, came the breakthrough. An offer from a company that not only recognized my potential but also valued the journey I had undertaken. Accepting the position felt like a validation of all the hard work, the sleepless nights, and the unwavering belief that I could rebuild my career.

As I prepared for my first day on the job, I felt a sense of accomplishment that was deeper than any I had felt before. Reestablishing my career was not just about finding employment; it was about rediscovering my purpose and proving to myself that I could rise above the challenges. The road ahead was still uncertain, but I was ready to face it with renewed vigor and a heart full of hope.

GAINING CONFIDENCE

Confidence has always been a fleeting concept in my life. It was like a shadow, sometimes visible, often elusive, and always dependent on the light around me. I remember the days when self-doubt was my constant companion, whispering in my ear, questioning my every move. Yet, as I navigated through the labyrinth of adversity, I discovered that confidence is not a gift bestowed upon the fortunate few; it is a skill that can be cultivated, nurtured, and grown.

The first step in gaining confidence was recognizing the small victories. In the face of overwhelming challenges, it's easy to overlook the minor successes that pave the way forward. I started by acknowledging the little things: completing a task I had been dreading, standing up for myself in a difficult conversation, or even getting out of bed on days when the weight of the world felt unbearable. These seemingly insignificant achievements became the building blocks of a more resilient self.

I also learned the importance of self-compassion. For years, I was my harshest critic, quick to point out my flaws and slow to recognize my strengths. This inner dialogue was not only unkind but also unproductive. It was a revelation to understand that treating myself with the same kindness and understanding that I offered to others could be transformative. I began to speak to myself with gentleness, forgiving my mistakes and celebrating my efforts. This shift in perspective was not immediate, but with time, it allowed me to see myself in a more positive light.

Another crucial element in building confidence was seeking out supportive relationships. The people we surround ourselves with can either lift us up or drag us down. I made a conscious effort to distance myself from those who fueled my insecurities and to cultivate connections with individuals who believed in me, even when I struggled to believe in myself. These supportive relationships provided a mirror in which I could see my potential reflected back at me, offering a perspective that was often clearer than my own.

Engaging in activities that pushed me out of my comfort zone was another key strategy. Confidence grows through experience, and experience often requires stepping into the unknown. I took on challenges that scared me, whether it was speaking in public, trying a new hobby, or traveling alone. Each new experience, regardless of the outcome, taught me something valuable about my capabilities and resilience. These moments of bravery, however small, accumulated over time, reinforcing my belief in myself.

Mindfulness and reflection also played a significant role in my journey toward confidence. Taking the time to reflect on my experiences, to understand what worked and what didn't, provided valuable insights. Mindfulness practices, such as meditation and journaling, helped me stay grounded and connected to my inner self. They allowed me to observe my thoughts and feelings without judgment, fostering a deeper sense of self-awareness and acceptance.

Confidence is not a destination but a continuous process of growth and self-discovery. It is built through a combination of self-awareness, supportive relationships, and the courage to step into the unknown. It requires patience, perseverance, and a willingness to celebrate both the small wins and the larger successes. Through this ongoing process, I have learned that confidence is not about never feeling fear or doubt; it is about moving forward despite those feelings, trusting in my ability to navigate whatever comes my way.

MOVING FORWARD

The path through adversity is often strewn with obstacles that test our resilience, patience, and determination. It is in these moments of struggle that the true essence of our character is revealed. As we navigate these challenges, we must remain mindful of the lessons learned and the growth achieved. This chapter is a reflection on how to integrate those lessons into our lives, ensuring that we not only survive but thrive.

It is essential to recognize the strength that has been cultivated through facing adversity. Each hurdle overcome is a testament to our ability to persevere, to push through pain and discomfort, and to emerge stronger on the other side. This newfound strength should be acknowledged and celebrated, as it forms the foundation upon which future successes will be built. By understanding our own capacity for resilience, we can approach future challenges with a renewed sense of confidence and determination.

Self-reflection plays a crucial role in this process. Taking the time to analyze our experiences allows us to identify patterns and behaviors that either hinder or help our progress. It is through this introspection that we can begin to make conscious choices about how we respond to difficulties. Are we prone to self-doubt, or do we draw on our inner strength to push forward? By recognizing these tendencies, we can work to cultivate a mindset that is more conducive to growth and success.

Another important aspect to consider is the support system that surrounds us. The people who stand by us during our darkest times often play a significant role in our ability to persevere. Acknowledging their contributions and expressing gratitude can strengthen these relationships, creating a network of support that will be invaluable in the face of future challenges. Additionally, being a source of support for others can provide a sense of purpose and fulfillment, further enhancing our own resilience.

The journey through adversity often requires us to adapt and change in ways we never anticipated. Embracing this change, rather than resisting it, can open up new opportunities for growth and development. Flexibility and adaptability are key traits that will serve us well in all areas of life. By remaining open to new experiences and perspectives, we can continue to evolve and improve, even in the face of adversity.

Setting realistic goals and creating actionable plans is another vital step in this process. By breaking down larger objectives into manageable tasks, we can maintain a sense of progress and achievement, even when faced with setbacks. This approach not only keeps us motivated but also allows us to celebrate small victories along the way, reinforcing our sense of accomplishment and reinforcing our determination to succeed.

It is also important to maintain a sense of balance in our lives. While striving for success and overcoming adversity are important, it is equally crucial to prioritize self-care and well-being. Taking time to rest, recharge, and engage in activities that bring joy and fulfillment can help prevent burnout and ensure that we have the energy and resilience needed to face future challenges.

Ultimately, the process of moving forward after adversity is a delicate balance of reflection, adaptation, and action. By acknowledging our strengths, learning from our experiences, and fostering a supportive network, we can continue to grow and thrive, no matter what challenges come our way. The journey through adversity is not just about survival; it is about transforming our struggles into opportunities for growth and becoming the best versions of ourselves.

Chapter 12: Reconnecting with Passion

FINDING WHAT MATTERS

When life throws curveballs, it often feels like being lost in a dense fog. The world becomes murky, and every step forward is hesitant, filled with uncertainty. It is in these moments that the essence of what truly matters begins to reveal itself, not through grand gestures or monumental events, but through the quiet, often overlooked details of our daily lives.

Reflecting on my own experiences, I remember a time when adversity seemed to shadow every corner of my existence. Days merged into nights, and the once clear distinctions between my aspirations and realities blurred. It was during these challenging periods that I began to notice the small things—the warmth of a morning sunbeam filtering through the window, the comforting aroma of freshly brewed coffee, the reassuring silence of a friend who simply sat with me. These seemingly insignificant moments became beacons, guiding me through the haze.

Adversity has a peculiar way of stripping away the superfluous. It acts as a sieve, allowing only the most essential elements of our lives to pass through. When faced with hardship, the distractions that once seemed so important—status, material wealth, fleeting pleasures—begin to pale in comparison to the simple, enduring connections and experiences that sustain us. It is in the midst of struggle that we start to discern the true value of relationships, the importance of self-care, and the power of resilience.

I recall a particular instance when I was at my lowest. A close friend reached out, not with words of advice or solutions, but with a simple gesture of presence. We sat in silence, the weight of my troubles heavy in the air, yet her quiet companionship spoke volumes. In that moment, I realized that what mattered most was not the resolution of my problems, but the unwavering support and understanding of those who cared for me.

Self-reflection during challenging times also brings clarity to our own strengths and passions. The adversity I faced pushed me to look inward, to reassess my goals and motivations. It was an uncomfortable process, peeling back layers of doubt and fear, but it led me to a deeper understanding of myself. I discovered a resilience I didn't know I possessed, and a renewed sense of purpose emerged from the depths of my struggles.

Moreover, adversity teaches us the significance of self-compassion. In the past, I was often my harshest critic, quick to judge my failures and shortcomings. However, enduring difficult times taught me to extend the same kindness and patience to myself that I so readily offered to others. This shift in perspective was transformative, allowing me to navigate challenges with a gentler, more forgiving approach.

Every challenge, every moment of hardship, holds within it the potential for profound insight and growth. While it is natural to seek out the grand narratives and life-changing epiphanies, often it is the quiet, unassuming moments that hold the key to understanding what truly matters. In the end, it is the accumulation of these small, significant experiences that shapes our journey through adversity, guiding us toward a more meaningful and fulfilled existence.

EMBRACING CREATIVITY

Creativity has always been an elusive force, dancing on the edges of my consciousness, waiting for moments of vulnerability to step forward. It's ironic, perhaps, that the times when life felt most challenging were the moments creativity seemed to surge forth with the most vigor. It's as if the very act of facing adversity cracked open a door to a deeper well of innovation and imagination.

Reflecting on these moments, I realize that creativity isn't just a skill or a talent; it's a lifeline. During periods of hardship, when the world seems bleak and unyielding, creative expression offers an escape, a way to reframe reality and find meaning amidst chaos. Whether through writing, painting, or simply daydreaming, allowing myself to dive into creative pursuits provided a sanctuary from the harshness of reality.

Not every creative endeavor resulted in a masterpiece, but that was never the point. The act of creating, of pouring my soul into something tangible, was cathartic. It allowed me to process emotions that words alone couldn't capture. Sometimes, a swirl of colors on a canvas spoke volumes more than any conversation could. Other times, a hastily scribbled poem became a vessel for my deepest fears and hopes.

It's fascinating how adversity can strip away the superficial layers of our existence, revealing the raw, unpolished core of who we are. In those stripped-down moments, creativity becomes a mirror, reflecting our innermost thoughts and feelings. It's a process of discovery, often leading to insights about ourselves that we might have otherwise overlooked.

Looking back, some of my most profound creative breakthroughs happened during periods of intense struggle. These were times when societal expectations and self-imposed limitations faded into the background, allowing a more authentic and uninhibited form of expression to emerge. The pressures and constraints of everyday life often stifle creativity, but adversity, with all its challenges, can paradoxically provide the freedom needed to explore new ideas and perspectives.

There is a certain beauty in creating something out of nothing, especially when that creation is born from a place of pain or difficulty. It's a testament to the resilience of the human spirit, a reminder that we can transform even the most challenging experiences into something meaningful and beautiful. This transformation is not just about the end product, but about the process itself—the journey of turning adversity into art, of finding light in the darkest of times.

In moments of reflection, I see how creativity has been a constant companion, guiding me through the labyrinth of life's challenges. It has taught me that there is always a way to reimagine our circumstances, to find new paths and possibilities. Creativity has shown me that even in the face of adversity, there is always room for growth, for innovation, and for hope.

As I continue to navigate the complexities of life, I hold onto the lessons that creativity has taught me. It's a reminder that within each of us lies an infinite well of potential, waiting to be tapped into, especially when we need it the most. This realization is both empowering and humbling, a testament to the enduring power of the human spirit to adapt, evolve, and create.

PASSION PROJECTS

As I navigated through the turbulent waters of my personal struggles, I found solace and strength in unexpected places. Among these sanctuaries were my passion projects, which emerged as more than just hobbies or ways to pass the time. They became lifelines, anchoring me and offering a sense of purpose that transcended the challenges I faced.

The first project that captured my heart was painting. With each brushstroke, I found a way to express emotions that words often failed to convey. The canvas became a mirror, reflecting my inner turmoil and moments of clarity. Through painting, I discovered a language that was uniquely mine, a silent conversation between my soul and the colors that danced before my eyes. This creative outlet allowed me to process my adversities in a way that felt both liberating and therapeutic.

Music was another passion that played a pivotal role in my journey. Learning to play the guitar was not just about mastering chords and melodies; it was about finding harmony in the chaos. Strumming the strings, I felt a connection to something greater than myself. Each note resonated with my experiences, transforming pain into beauty. Music became a refuge, a place where I could lose myself and, in doing so, find fragments of my true self that had been buried under layers of hardship.

Writing, too, offered a sanctuary. Penning down my thoughts and stories allowed me to make sense of the whirlwind around me. It was through writing that I could dissect my feelings, understand my fears, and celebrate my victories, no matter how small. The act of writing was both a release and a revelation, a way to document my growth and resilience. It provided a structured way to reflect on my experiences and draw lessons from them, turning adversity into a source of wisdom.

Gardening became a silent yet powerful teacher. Tending to plants, watching them grow and flourish, mirrored my own journey of healing and renewal. The patience required to nurture a garden taught me to be patient with myself. Each bloom and each harvest was a testament to the power of persistence and care. The garden became a metaphor for life itself, with its cycles of growth, decay, and rebirth. It reminded me that, even in the face of adversity, there is always potential for new beginnings.

Engaging in these passion projects was not just about distraction; it was about transformation. They provided a way to channel my energy, to create something meaningful out of the chaos. They taught me valuable lessons about resilience, creativity, and the importance of nurturing one's soul. Through them, I found a way to reclaim my narrative, to define myself not by the adversities I faced, but by the passions I pursued and the dreams I dared to chase.

These projects became a testament to the human spirit's capacity for growth and renewal. They were reminders that, even in the darkest of times, there is light to be found and beauty to be created. They were my companions and guides, leading me through the labyrinth of my struggles and towards a place of hope and possibility. In the end, it was through these passions that I discovered the strength to not just survive, but to thrive.

BALANCING WORK AND PASSION

I remember the days when the clock seemed to tick louder, reminding me of deadlines, meetings, and the never-ending cycle of tasks. My mind would often drift to my passions, those activities that made my heart race with excitement and filled my soul with a sense of fulfillment. The tug-of-war between work and passion was relentless, each side demanding its share of my time and energy. It was a dance that required careful choreography, a balance that seemed almost impossible to achieve.

In the midst of career pressures, the spark of creativity and passion often flickered, struggling to stay alight. The corporate world, with its rigid structures and relentless pace, left little room for the spontaneity and freedom that passion demands. Yet, it was in those stolen moments, a few minutes here and there, that I found solace and rejuvenation. A quick sketch during a lunch break, a melody hummed on the way home, or a paragraph written in the quiet of the night. These were the threads that wove my passion into the fabric of my daily life, a reminder that it was still very much a part of me.

The challenge was not just about finding time, but about giving myself permission to pursue these passions without guilt. Society often places a premium on productivity and efficiency, leaving little room for what might be deemed as 'frivolous' pursuits. Yet, I came to realize that these so-called frivolities were essential to my well-being. They were not distractions, but rather, they were the lifelines that kept me afloat amidst the sea of responsibilities.

There were moments of clarity, when I understood that my work and my passions were not mutually exclusive. They could coexist, each enriching the other. The skills and discipline I honed in my professional life often found their way into my creative endeavors, while the joy and fulfillment from my passions spilled over into my work, infusing it with a renewed sense of purpose. It was a symbiotic relationship, one that required constant nurturing and adjustment.

I learned to set boundaries, to carve out sacred spaces of time dedicated solely to my passions. These were non-negotiable, a sanctuary where I could lose myself in the act of creation. It was in these moments that I found a deeper connection to myself, a reminder of who I was beyond the titles and roles assigned by my career. This balance was not a static state, but a dynamic process, one that required continuous effort and mindfulness.

The journey of balancing work and passion was not without its struggles. There were times when one overshadowed the other, leading to frustration and burnout. Yet, each setback was a lesson, a reminder to recalibrate and prioritize what truly mattered. It was in these moments of imbalance that I discovered the resilience and adaptability within me, the ability to navigate the complexities of life with grace and determination.

Reflecting on this journey, I am filled with gratitude for the lessons learned and the growth experienced. The balance between work and passion is a delicate dance, one that requires patience, perseverance, and a deep understanding of oneself. It is a journey of self-discovery, a testament to the power of following one's heart amidst the demands of the world.

LIVING WITH PURPOSE

Purpose often reveals itself in the most unexpected places. There were countless moments when I felt lost, grappling with the weight of my challenges. It seemed as if adversity had built an impenetrable wall around me. But within those very walls, I found a glimmer of clarity. The struggles, the pain, and the seemingly insurmountable obstacles began to serve as mirrors, reflecting not just my weaknesses, but also my strengths and deep-seated desires.

In navigating through turbulent times, I discovered that purpose isn't a grand, predefined path. It's a series of small, deliberate choices made in the face of adversity. Every setback became a lesson, every challenge a stepping stone. The purpose was not something I found; it was something I built, piece by piece, through resilience and reflection.

There was a day when I stood at a crossroads, overwhelmed by the weight of my circumstances. I asked myself what truly mattered. What did I want my life to stand for? The answers didn't come immediately. They were buried under layers of doubt and fear. But as I began to peel back those layers, a clearer picture started to form. I realized that my purpose was intertwined with my passion for helping others navigate their own adversities.

The act of sharing my story, of being vulnerable and honest about my struggles, became a powerful tool. It was through this sharing that I found a deeper connection with others and, in turn, with myself. Each time I spoke of my experiences, I felt a sense of liberation. It was as if the very act of articulating my journey allowed me to reclaim my narrative, to shape it into something meaningful.

Living with purpose doesn't mean that adversity ceases to exist. On the contrary, it means facing challenges with a renewed sense of determination and clarity. It means understanding that every hurdle is an opportunity to reinforce one's commitment to their goals. There were days when the weight of my challenges felt unbearable, but the knowledge that I was working towards something greater gave me the strength to persevere.

Reflection became a cornerstone of my daily life. I would often sit in solitude, contemplating the events of the day, the choices I made, and the lessons learned. This practice of introspection allowed me to stay aligned with my purpose, to ensure that my actions were in harmony with my values and aspirations.

Purpose is not a destination but a continuous journey. It's about finding meaning in every moment, in every action, no matter how small. It's about recognizing that even in the face of adversity, there is a deeper significance to our struggles. Each challenge is a testament to our resilience, each setback a reminder of our strength.

In the end, living with purpose is about embracing the entirety of our experience, the highs and the lows, the triumphs and the tribulations. It's about understanding that our purpose is not defined by the absence of adversity, but by our response to it. Through every challenge, we find an opportunity to grow, to learn, and to reaffirm our commitment to the path we have chosen.

Chapter 13: The Power of Reflection

The past holds a mirror to who we are today, reflecting both the shadows and the light of our experiences. Growing up, my world was a tapestry of challenges, each thread woven with a lesson that would later define my character. The early years were anything but easy, marked by trials that seemed insurmountable at the time. Yet, it was within these very trials that the seeds of resilience were sown.

As a child, I often found myself grappling with feelings of inadequacy. The weight of expectations, both self-imposed and external, hung heavily on my shoulders. It wasn't just about meeting academic standards or excelling in extracurricular activities; it was about proving to myself and others that I was capable. The pressure was relentless, and there were moments when the burden felt too much to bear.

School was a battlefield of sorts. Each day presented its own set of challenges, from navigating social hierarchies to striving for academic excellence. There were days when I felt like an outsider, struggling to fit into a mold that seemed to constantly shift. The desire to belong was strong, but so was the fear of losing myself in the process. Balancing these conflicting emotions was a delicate act, one that required a level of introspection I wasn't always prepared for.

Family dynamics added another layer of complexity. My family, though loving, had their own struggles and expectations. Their dreams for me were both a source of motivation and a cause of anxiety. I wanted to make them proud, to live up to the aspirations they had for me. But there were times when their dreams felt like chains, binding me to a path that wasn't entirely my own. It took years to understand that their hopes were born out of love, even if they sometimes felt like pressure.

Friendships, too, were a mixed bag. There were those who stood by me, offering support and understanding. But there were also those who seemed to revel in my struggles, using them as a measure of their own success. Learning to discern true friends from fair-weather ones was a painful yet necessary lesson. It taught me the value of loyalty and the importance of surrounding myself with people who genuinely cared.

Reflecting on these early experiences, it's clear that each challenge, no matter how daunting, played a crucial role in shaping who I am. The adversity I faced wasn't just an obstacle to overcome; it was a catalyst for growth. It taught me to dig deep, to find strength in vulnerability, and to never underestimate my own resilience.

Looking back, I see a younger version of myself, navigating a complex world with a blend of fear and determination. The road was rough, often filled with unexpected twists and turns. But with each step, I grew stronger, more self-aware, and more capable of facing whatever lay ahead. The past, with all its trials, was not just a series of unfortunate events but a foundation upon which I built my strength and character.

In those moments of reflection, I realize that adversity was not my enemy but my teacher. It showed me that strength is not the absence of struggle but the ability to persist through it. Each challenge was a lesson in disguise, preparing me for the person I would eventually become. The journey was far from easy, but it was undeniably transformative.

LESSONS LEARNED

Reflecting on the myriad experiences of my life, it's evident that adversity has been both a harsh teacher and a benevolent guide. The lessons I've gathered are not merely intellectual understandings but visceral truths, etched deeply into my being. Each challenge, each setback, has imparted wisdom that no textbook could ever convey.

One profound realization is the importance of resilience. It's not just about bouncing back from difficulties but about the transformation that occurs in the process. Resilience is cultivated through the continual act of facing discomfort and uncertainty head-on. It's about developing a mindset that sees obstacles not as insurmountable walls but as opportunities for growth. This shift in perspective has allowed me to navigate life's tumultuous waters with a sense of purpose and determination.

Another significant lesson is the value of vulnerability. Society often glorifies strength and stoicism, but true strength lies in the courage to be vulnerable. Admitting fears, acknowledging pain, and expressing emotions are not signs of weakness but of profound self-awareness and authenticity. Embracing vulnerability has deepened my connections with others, fostering empathy and understanding. It has also allowed me to be more compassionate towards myself, recognizing that imperfection is an intrinsic part of the human experience.

The importance of adaptability cannot be overstated. Life is inherently unpredictable, and the ability to adapt to changing circumstances is crucial. This flexibility has taught me to let go of rigid expectations and to approach situations with an open mind. It has encouraged me to be creative in finding solutions and to remain hopeful even when the path ahead is unclear. Adaptability has reinforced the notion that while we may not control every event, we can control our responses and attitudes.

Gratitude has emerged as a cornerstone of my outlook. In the face of adversity, it's easy to focus on what is lacking or what has been lost. However, cultivating a habit of gratitude shifts the focus to what remains and what can be appreciated. This practice has illuminated the small joys and blessings that often go unnoticed. Gratitude has become a source of strength, providing a steady anchor amidst life's storms.

Another lesson that stands out is the significance of community and support. Facing challenges alone can be daunting, but the presence of a supportive network can make a world of difference. Whether it's family, friends, or even strangers who lend a helping hand, the connections we forge in times of adversity are invaluable. They remind us that we are not isolated in our struggles and that collective strength can overcome individual hardships.

Lastly, the journey through adversity has underscored the importance of self-reflection. Taking the time to introspect and understand one's reactions, choices, and motivations has been instrumental in personal growth. Self-reflection has provided clarity, helping me to recognize patterns, identify areas for improvement, and celebrate progress. It has been a tool for continuous learning, allowing me to evolve and adapt with each new challenge.

These lessons, born from the crucible of adversity, have shaped my character and outlook on life. They serve as a testament to the transformative power of facing challenges with courage, openness, and a willingness to learn. Through adversity, I have discovered strengths I never knew I possessed and have grown in ways I never imagined possible.

GROWTH THROUGH REFLECTION

The moments of stillness often reveal more about ourselves than the bustling chaos of our daily lives. It is within these quiet interludes that we can truly examine the intricate tapestry of our experiences, especially those woven with threads of adversity. Reflecting on the trials we've faced not only illuminates the lessons hidden within them but also catalyzes our personal growth.

The process of growth through reflection is neither linear nor immediate. It demands patience and a willingness to confront the uncomfortable truths that lie beneath the surface. Each setback, each moment of despair, offers a unique opportunity to delve deeper into our psyche, to understand our reactions, and to recognize the patterns that govern our behavior. By doing so, we begin to dismantle the barriers that adversity constructs around us.

Consider the times when you felt overwhelmed by life's challenges. In those instances, it is easy to succumb to a sense of helplessness, to allow the weight of the world to anchor you in a state of inertia. However, by taking a step back and reflecting on these moments, we can shift our perspective. What initially appears as insurmountable can be reframed as a series of manageable tasks. This shift in viewpoint is not merely a mental exercise but a profound transformation that equips us with the resilience needed to navigate future obstacles.

Reflection also fosters a deeper understanding of our strengths and weaknesses. When adversity strikes, our immediate reaction is often a testament to our innate capabilities. By analyzing these reactions, we can identify the skills and attributes that aided us in overcoming the challenge. Simultaneously, we can pinpoint the areas where we faltered, providing us with a roadmap for personal development. This dual awareness is crucial for cultivating a balanced sense of self, one that acknowledges both our potential and our limitations.

Moreover, growth through reflection nurtures empathy and compassion, not only towards others but towards ourselves. It is easy to be self-critical, to dwell on our perceived failures and shortcomings. Yet, by reflecting on our experiences with a gentle and understanding lens, we learn to forgive ourselves. This self-compassion is vital for fostering a healthy mindset, one that encourages continuous growth rather than being mired in self-doubt.

The act of reflection also connects us to a broader narrative. Our individual struggles, while deeply personal, are part of the collective human experience. By recognizing this interconnectedness, we find solace in the knowledge that we are not alone in our journey. This shared understanding can be a powerful source of motivation and strength, reminding us that adversity, while challenging, is a universal catalyst for growth.

In the grand tapestry of life, each thread of adversity weaves a story of resilience, courage, and transformation. By embracing the practice of reflection, we not only honor our past experiences but also pave the way for a more enlightened and empowered future. Through introspection, we transform our adversities into stepping stones, guiding us towards a more profound understanding of ourselves and our place in the world.

APPLYING WISDOM

Navigating the turbulent waters of adversity often feels like steering a boat in the dark. However, there comes a moment when the lessons learned from past storms become our guiding lights. Reflecting on those difficult times, wisdom emerges not as an abstract concept but as a practical tool, a beacon of hope and direction.

In the quiet aftermath of a challenge, when the immediate chaos has subsided, there lies an opportunity to sift through the experiences. Each trial, each setback, holds a lesson, an insight waiting to be uncovered. It's in these moments of introspection that wisdom begins to take shape. It's not about having all the answers, but about asking the right questions. What did this experience teach me about myself? How can I use this knowledge to navigate future challenges?

The application of wisdom requires a delicate balance of reflection and action. It's about integrating the insights gained into our daily lives. This can be as simple as recognizing the importance of patience when facing a seemingly insurmountable obstacle or understanding the value of resilience in the face of repeated setbacks. These realizations, though seemingly small, can profoundly impact our approach to adversity.

Consider the story of a craftsman who, after years of honing his skills, understands the grain of the wood he works with. He knows when to apply pressure and when to ease off. Similarly, wisdom teaches us to discern the nuances of our challenges. It helps us identify when to push forward and when to step back, when to seek help and when to trust in our own abilities.

One of the most powerful aspects of wisdom is its ability to transform our perspective. Adversity, when viewed through the lens of wisdom, becomes less of a burden and more of an opportunity for growth. It shifts our focus from what we've lost to what we've gained, from the pain endured to the strength developed. This shift in perspective is not about denying the difficulty of the experience but about recognizing and valuing the growth it catalyzes.

In practical terms, applying wisdom might involve setting boundaries to protect our well-being, seeking out mentors who can offer guidance, or simply taking a moment each day to reflect on our progress. It's about making conscious choices that align with the insights we've gained. These choices, though sometimes challenging, pave the way for a more resilient and empowered approach to life's inevitable difficulties.

Moreover, wisdom encourages us to cultivate a sense of gratitude. Even in the darkest times, there are moments of light, lessons learned, and strengths discovered. By acknowledging and appreciating these, we foster a more positive outlook and build a reservoir of resilience that can be drawn upon in future trials.

The journey of applying wisdom is ongoing. It's a continuous process of learning, reflecting, and adapting. It's about staying open to new insights, even when they come from the most unexpected places. Each experience, each challenge, adds another layer to our understanding, guiding us toward a more thoughtful and intentional way of living.

In the end, wisdom is the gentle whisper that reminds us we are capable, resilient, and ever-evolving. It's the quiet strength that steadies us in the face of adversity, the inner compass that guides us through the storm. And as we continue to navigate our path, it's this wisdom that illuminates the way forward, offering hope and clarity in even the darkest of times.

A BETTER VERSION OF MYSELF

The morning light filtered through the curtains, casting a warm glow on the room. As I looked in the mirror, I saw not just my reflection, but a story of growth and transformation. There was a time when the person staring back at me seemed unrecognizable, shrouded in doubt and uncertainty. Those days felt like a lifetime ago, yet the lessons learned remain vivid.

Adversity has a peculiar way of shaping us, chiseling away at the rough edges to reveal a more refined version of ourselves. The challenges faced were not merely obstacles, but opportunities disguised in hardship. Each struggle, each moment of despair, was a stepping stone to becoming someone stronger, more resilient. It's fascinating how the darkest moments often lead to the most profound revelations.

The process of self-improvement isn't linear. There were days filled with progress, where the horizon seemed within reach, and others where the weight of setbacks felt insurmountable. It was during these lows that the true test of character emerged. The ability to rise, to push forward despite the odds, is where real growth happens. It's in these moments that one discovers an inner strength previously unknown.

Reflection played a crucial role in this transformation. Taking the time to look inward, to understand the motivations and fears that drive actions, provided clarity. It's easy to get lost in the noise of everyday life, to let the external world dictate one's sense of self-worth. But true growth comes from within, from a place of self-awareness and acceptance.

Recognizing flaws and acknowledging mistakes became a powerful tool for change.

Support from loved ones also made a significant difference. Their unwavering belief, even when my own faith wavered, provided a foundation to build upon. It's often said that we are the sum of the people around us, and in this journey, their influence was undeniable. Their encouragement, their own stories of overcoming adversity, served as a beacon of hope.

Alongside personal reflection and support, setting tangible goals was instrumental. Small, achievable milestones created a sense of accomplishment, fueling the drive to keep moving forward. Each success, no matter how minor, was a reminder of the progress made and a motivator to continue striving for better.

One of the most profound changes was shifting the mindset from seeing adversity as a burden to viewing it as a catalyst for growth. This perspective shift transformed challenges into opportunities for learning and self-discovery. It wasn't about avoiding difficulties but embracing them as a crucial part of the journey towards self-improvement.

As I stand here today, I see a version of myself that is more confident, more self-assured. The road was far from easy, filled with twists and turns, but each step was a testament to the power of resilience. The person in the mirror now reflects not just the scars of past battles, but the strength and wisdom gained from them. This journey of transformation is ongoing, a continuous process of becoming a better version of oneself. Every day brings new challenges and new opportunities for growth, and with each one, the reflection in the mirror becomes clearer, more defined, and undeniably stronger.

Chapter 14: Embracing the Future

HOPE AND OPTIMISM

In the midst of life's turbulent storms, I often found myself clinging to the fragile threads of hope and optimism. These weren't just abstract concepts but lifelines that kept me afloat when the waves of adversity threatened to pull me under. Reflecting on my experiences, I realized that hope and optimism were not mere feelings but powerful forces that shaped my reality.

There were moments when everything seemed bleak, and the weight of challenges felt insurmountable. During these times, hope served as a beacon, a distant light that guided me through the darkness. It was the quiet, persistent belief that things could get better, even when evidence suggested otherwise. I remember sitting alone in my room, feeling the crushing weight of despair, and yet, somewhere deep within, a tiny flicker of hope refused to be extinguished. It whispered that tomorrow could bring new possibilities, new opportunities for growth and healing.

Optimism, on the other hand, was the lens through which I chose to view my circumstances. It wasn't about ignoring the harsh realities or pretending that everything was perfect. Instead, it was about finding the silver linings, the lessons hidden within the struggles. I learned that optimism was a practice, a deliberate choice to focus on the positives, however small they might be. It was about celebrating the little victories, the steps forward, no matter how minuscule they seemed.

I recall a particularly challenging period in my life when everything appeared to be falling apart. My career was in jeopardy, personal relationships were strained, and my health was deteriorating. It was during this time that I discovered the profound impact of maintaining an optimistic outlook. I started journaling, documenting not just my struggles but also the moments of joy, the acts of kindness, and the progress, however slow. This practice didn't change my circumstances overnight, but it transformed my perception. It allowed me to see that amidst the chaos, there were still reasons to be grateful, still moments of beauty and connection.

Hope and optimism also played a crucial role in my interactions with others. I noticed that when I approached situations with a hopeful and optimistic mindset, it had a ripple effect. My positivity often inspired those around me, creating a supportive and encouraging environment. It wasn't about being unrealistically cheerful but about fostering a sense of possibility and resilience.

Looking back, I understand that hope and optimism were not just survival mechanisms but catalysts for growth. They empowered me to take risks, to pursue dreams, and to navigate the uncertainties of life with a sense of purpose. They taught me that while I couldn't always control my circumstances, I could control my response to them.

The journey through adversity was not linear, and there were times when hope and optimism seemed elusive. Yet, it was during these moments of struggle that I learned their true value. They were not guarantees of a trouble-free life but companions that made the challenges bearable, the victories sweeter, and the journey meaningful. Through hope and optimism, I discovered a resilience within myself that I never knew existed, a strength that propelled me forward even when the path was unclear.

FUTURE PLANS

As I look ahead, the horizon is both daunting and exhilarating. The path that has led me here has been riddled with obstacles, each one a lesson in resilience and self-discovery. Reflecting on the past, it becomes clear that adversity has shaped not just who I am, but also what I aim to achieve moving forward.

In the quiet moments of introspection, I often find myself contemplating the kind of future I wish to build. It's not just about personal success or achieving milestones; it's about creating a life that resonates with the values and lessons learned through trials. There's a profound desire to channel the strength garnered from past struggles into meaningful endeavors. These plans are not just aspirations; they are commitments to a life of purpose.

One of the primary goals is to invest in personal growth continuously. The learning never stops, and the thirst for knowledge has only intensified with time. Whether through formal education, reading, or engaging with diverse perspectives, the aim is to cultivate a mind that is both curious and critical. This intellectual journey is not just for self-improvement but also to better understand and contribute to the world around me.

Another significant aspect of future plans revolves around relationships. The experiences have taught me the invaluable nature of connections—both familial and social. Strengthening these bonds and nurturing new ones is a priority. It's about being present, offering support, and finding joy in shared moments. Relationships are the bedrock of a fulfilling life, and they require time, effort, and genuine care.

Professionally, the aim is to align work with passion. The challenges faced have underscored the importance of finding meaning in what one does. It's not merely about financial stability but about engaging in work that feels impactful. This could mean pursuing a career that aligns with personal values or perhaps venturing into avenues that promote social good. The objective is to find a balance where work is not just a means to an end but a fulfilling part of life.

There's also a deep-seated commitment to giving back. The adversities encountered have instilled a sense of empathy and a desire to support others who might be facing similar struggles. This could manifest through community service, mentorship, or any form of outreach that can make a difference. The aim is to be a beacon of hope, just as others have been for me during tough times.

Health and well-being are also pivotal in these plans. The physical and mental toll of enduring hardships has highlighted the necessity of self-care. Prioritizing health, both physical and mental, is not just about longevity but about living a quality life. This involves regular exercise, mindful eating, and perhaps most importantly, ensuring mental peace through practices like meditation or therapy.

Travel and exploration remain on the agenda, not just for leisure but for the enrichment that comes from experiencing different cultures and environments. There's a world out there filled with stories, lessons, and beauty waiting to be discovered. Each new place visited is an opportunity to learn, grow, and find inspiration.

Looking forward, the future is a canvas, painted with the hues of past experiences and the aspirations for what lies ahead. It's a blend of dreams and realities, of plans meticulously laid out and the flexibility to adapt as life unfolds. The road ahead is unknown, but it's approached with a heart fortified by past adversities and a mind eager to embrace whatever comes next.

BUILDING RESILIENCE

Reflecting on the myriad challenges that life presents, it becomes evident that resilience is not just an innate trait but a skill that can be cultivated. My own experiences have taught me that resilience is less about bouncing back to a previous state and more about evolving into a stronger version of oneself. The process of building resilience is akin to forging steel; it requires heat, pressure, and time.

One of the first lessons I learned about resilience was through personal setbacks. It was during these moments of vulnerability that I discovered the importance of perspective. Shifting my viewpoint from seeing obstacles as insurmountable to viewing them as opportunities for growth was transformative. This mental shift doesn't eliminate adversity but equips us with the fortitude to navigate through it. I found that keeping a journal helped me articulate my thoughts and emotions, providing clarity and fostering a sense of control over my circumstances.

Another cornerstone of resilience is the support system we build around us. The significance of relationships cannot be overstated. Friends, family, mentors, and even acquaintances can provide the emotional scaffolding necessary to withstand life's storms. There were countless times when a simple word of encouragement from a loved one acted as a lifeline. It's crucial to recognize that seeking help is not a sign of weakness but a testament to our humanity and interconnectedness.

Mindfulness and self-care also play pivotal roles in fostering resilience. In the hustle and bustle of daily life, it's easy to neglect our mental and physical well-being. I learned the hard way that pushing through without taking time to recharge only leads to burnout. Practices such as meditation, exercise, and even hobbies can serve as vital outlets for stress and anxiety. These activities not only rejuvenate the mind and body but also build a reserve of inner strength that can be drawn upon in times of need.

Resilience is also about adaptability. Life rarely goes according to plan, and the ability to pivot and adjust is essential. I recall a period when my professional life was in turmoil. Instead of clinging to a rigid path, I explored alternative routes and discovered new passions and opportunities. This flexibility not only mitigated the impact of the setback but opened doors I hadn't previously considered.

Failures and mistakes, though often painful, are invaluable teachers. Embracing them with a mindset geared towards learning rather than self-criticism can significantly enhance resilience. Each failure is a lesson in disguise, offering insights that contribute to personal and professional growth. I made it a point to reflect on my missteps, identify the lessons within, and apply them moving forward.

Lastly, having a sense of purpose can act as a guiding star through adversity. Knowing why we do what we do provides the motivation to persevere even when the going gets tough. For me, reconnecting with my core values and long-term goals provided the impetus to keep pushing forward despite numerous setbacks.

Resilience is not a destination but an ongoing process, a continuous journey of self-discovery and growth. It's about building a toolkit of strategies and mindsets that enable us to face adversity with courage and grace. Through reflection, support, self-care, adaptability, learning from failures, and a sense of purpose, we can develop the resilience needed to navigate life's inevitable challenges.

ADAPTING TO CHANGE

Change, as we know it, is an inevitable force, an uninvited guest that often arrives unannounced, disrupting our carefully laid plans. It is a master sculptor, chiseling away at the granite of our existence, shaping us into forms we could never have imagined. Reflecting on my own experiences, I realize that change has been a constant companion, teaching me lessons that no book or mentor could impart.

In the midst of adversity, change often appears as a formidable adversary. It challenges our routines, questions our beliefs, and forces us to confront our deepest fears. Yet, it is in these moments of upheaval that we discover our true strength. I recall a time when I was navigating a particularly tumultuous period in my life. The familiar ground beneath my feet seemed to crumble, and I was left grappling with uncertainty. It was during this period that I learned the importance of flexibility and resilience.

Flexibility, I discovered, is not merely about bending without breaking; it is about embracing the fluidity of life. It is about understanding that rigidity can lead to our undoing, while adaptability can be our saving grace. I began to see change not as an enemy, but as a catalyst for growth. Each challenge presented an opportunity to learn, to evolve, and to become a better version of myself.

Resilience, on the other hand, is the quiet strength that lies within us, often dormant until called upon by adversity. It is the ability to bounce back, to rise from the ashes of our failures and forge ahead with renewed determination. I found that resilience is not about never falling, but about rising each time we do. It is about finding the courage to face change head-on, even when the odds seem insurmountable.

Through these experiences, I also learned the value of mindfulness. In the chaos of change, it is easy to become overwhelmed, to lose sight of our goals and succumb to anxiety. Mindfulness, however, offers a sanctuary. It allows us to remain grounded, to find clarity amidst the confusion. By focusing on the present moment, we can navigate the stormy seas of change with a sense of calm and purpose.

Support systems, too, play a crucial role in our ability to adapt. Friends, family, mentors – these are the pillars that hold us up when we falter. They provide us with the strength to persevere, the wisdom to make informed decisions, and the comfort to know that we are not alone. In my own journey, I have been fortunate to have a network of supportive individuals who have stood by me through thick and thin. Their encouragement and guidance have been invaluable, reminding me that even in the darkest of times, there is light to be found.

As I reflect on the lessons learned from adapting to change, I am reminded of the words of Charles Darwin: "It is not the strongest of the species that survive, nor the most intelligent, but the one most responsive to change." These words resonate deeply, for they encapsulate the essence of what it means to thrive in the face of adversity. Change, with all its unpredictability, is a powerful teacher. It compels us to grow, to innovate, and to become more resilient. And in doing so, it reveals the true depth of our potential.

CONTINUING THE JOURNEY

As I look back on the myriad of challenges that life has presented, I realize that each obstacle was not merely a roadblock but a stepping stone. The path has been winding, filled with unexpected detours, yet every twist and turn has contributed to my growth. Reflecting on these experiences, I see how they have shaped my character, tested my resolve, and ultimately strengthened my spirit.

In moments of hardship, it is easy to feel overwhelmed and defeated. The weight of adversity can seem unbearable, casting a shadow over any glimmer of hope. However, it is precisely in these dark times that the light within us can shine the brightest. By confronting our struggles head-on, we discover inner reserves of strength and resilience that we never knew we possessed. Each trial becomes an opportunity to learn more about ourselves, to dig deeper and to rise stronger.

The wisdom gained from overcoming difficulties is invaluable. It teaches us patience, perseverance, and empathy. We learn to appreciate the small victories, to celebrate progress no matter how incremental. We begin to understand that setbacks are not failures; they are part of the process. They teach us humility and the importance of persistence. With each challenge faced and conquered, our confidence grows, and we become more adept at navigating future obstacles.

Connection with others also plays a crucial role in weathering life's storms. Sharing our experiences with those who have faced similar trials fosters a sense of solidarity and understanding. It reminds us that we are not alone in our struggles. The support and encouragement from friends, family, and even strangers can provide the strength needed to keep moving forward. Moreover, by opening up about our own experiences, we can offer hope and inspiration to others who may be facing their own battles.

Self-reflection is another essential aspect of moving forward. Taking the time to assess our actions, reactions, and decisions allows us to gain insights into our behavior. It helps us identify patterns, recognize areas for improvement, and celebrate our growth. Through introspection, we can better understand our motivations and fears, enabling us to make more informed choices in the future.

As we continue on this path, it is important to remain open to change and to embrace the unknown. Life is unpredictable, and clinging to the past or fearing the future can hinder our progress. By maintaining a flexible mindset, we can adapt to new circumstances and seize opportunities that may arise. It is through this openness to change that we can continue to grow and evolve.

Ultimately, the experiences we face and the lessons we learn along the way contribute to a richer, more fulfilling life. The trials and tribulations that once seemed insurmountable become the very experiences that define us. They remind us of our resilience, our capacity for growth, and our ability to overcome. With each step taken, we move closer to becoming the best version of ourselves, ready to face whatever challenges lie ahead with courage and determination.

In this ongoing process of growth and self-discovery, we find meaning and purpose. We learn to trust ourselves and to have faith in our abilities. And as we look forward, we do so with a sense of hope and confidence, knowing that we are capable of handling whatever comes our way. The path may not always be smooth, but it is ours to navigate, and with each step, we continue to move forward, ever stronger and wiser.

Chapter 15: A Testament to Strength

UNYIELDING SPIRIT

As I sit by the window, the rain tapping gently against the glass, I find myself reflecting on the moments that have shaped me. The quiet persistence of the rain mirrors the tenacity required to navigate life's challenges. Adversity is an uninvited guest, often arriving without warning and overstaying its welcome. Yet, it is in these moments of struggle that we uncover the depths of our resilience.

I recall a time when the weight of the world seemed too much to bear. It was a period marked by uncertainty and fear, where every step forward felt like wading through quicksand. The temptation to surrender to despair was ever-present, whispering insidiously that the fight was futile. But somewhere deep within, a flicker of defiance refused to be extinguished. That flicker, though small, was a beacon of hope.

The human spirit is a remarkable force, capable of enduring far more than we often give it credit for. It is not the absence of fear or pain that defines strength, but the ability to continue despite them. This realization dawned on me gradually, like the first light of dawn breaking through the darkness. It is easy to forget, in moments of hardship, that we possess an inherent capacity to overcome.

Support from loved ones played a crucial role during this time. Their unwavering belief in my ability to persevere served as a lifeline. Words of encouragement, acts of kindness, and the simple act of listening provided the scaffolding needed to rebuild my confidence. It became clear that while the battle was mine to fight, I was not alone in it.

There were days when progress seemed nonexistent, where the effort expended felt disproportionate to the gains made. Yet, each small victory, no matter how insignificant it seemed at the time, was a testament to the power of persistence. It is in these incremental steps that true growth occurs. The path to recovery is seldom linear; it is a series of peaks and valleys, each contributing to the tapestry of our experience.

In retrospect, the adversity faced was not merely an obstacle but a crucible that forged a stronger, more resilient version of myself. It stripped away the superficial, revealing the core of what truly mattered. Values such as empathy, gratitude, and humility were no longer abstract concepts but lived experiences. The trials endured became a source of wisdom, a wellspring from which to draw strength in future challenges.

As the rain continues to fall, I am reminded that growth often comes from the most unexpected places. Adversity, while unwelcome, has the potential to be a powerful teacher. It demands that we look within, to confront our vulnerabilities and rediscover our strengths. It is through this process that we develop an unyielding spirit, one that refuses to be broken by the trials of life.

In these quiet moments of reflection, I am grateful for the journey. The struggles faced have not only shaped who I am but have also provided a profound appreciation for the resilience of the human spirit. Each challenge met and overcome is a testament to the indomitable will that resides within us all. The rain outside may be relentless, but so too is the spirit that rises to meet it.

INSPIRING OTHERS

Reflecting on the experiences that have shaped us, we often find that our struggles and triumphs offer profound lessons not just for ourselves, but for others as well. Adversity, in its many forms, has a way of molding us into more resilient and compassionate beings. It is through our own battles and victories that we can spark a light in those who may be walking a similar path.

I recall a time when I faced significant challenges, and it was the stories of others who had conquered their own difficulties that kept me going. These narratives were not just tales of overcoming but were beacons of hope, illustrating that resilience is not just a personal trait but a collective strength. Hearing about someone else's journey through hardship can be incredibly empowering. It helps us understand that we are not alone, and that our struggles, while unique, are part of a larger human experience.

In sharing our stories, we offer a gift to others. Our experiences, whether they involve personal loss, professional setbacks, or physical challenges, become a testament to the human spirit's unyielding nature. When we speak of our struggles and how we navigated them, we provide a blueprint for others to follow. This act of sharing is not about boasting or seeking sympathy; it is about creating a connection, a bridge between our experiences and those of others.

One of the most powerful ways to inspire others is by being authentic. Authenticity resonates because it is real and relatable. When we are honest about our fears, our failures, and our moments of doubt, we give others permission to acknowledge their own vulnerabilities. This authenticity fosters a sense of community and belonging, which is crucial when facing adversity. Knowing that someone else has been through what we are currently experiencing can be incredibly validating and motivating.

Encouragement also plays a crucial role in inspiring others. Simple words of support and affirmation can have a profound impact. Sometimes, people just need to hear that they are capable, that they have the strength to overcome their challenges. Offering a listening ear, a kind word, or a piece of advice can make a world of difference. It is these small acts of kindness and support that often provide the courage needed to face the next obstacle.

Leading by example is another powerful way to inspire. When others see us navigating our difficulties with grace and determination, they are often inspired to do the same. Our actions speak louder than words, and living our lives in a way that reflects our values and resilience can be a powerful motivator for others. It shows that it is possible to live a fulfilling life even in the face of significant challenges.

In the end, our adversities can become a source of inspiration for others. By sharing our stories, being authentic, offering encouragement, and leading by example, we can help others find their own strength and resilience. Through our experiences, we have the power to inspire, uplift, and empower those around us, creating a ripple effect that extends far beyond our immediate circle.

LEGACY OF RESILIENCE

The echoes of adversity have a way of etching themselves into the core of one's being, leaving indelible marks that shape the contours of our existence. Reflecting on the myriad challenges that life has presented, I find myself in awe of the resilience that has been forged in the crucible of hardship. It is a resilience that is not merely a response to adversity but a profound transformation that redefines the essence of who we are.

As I look back, I realize that resilience is not an innate trait but a cultivated strength. It is the product of countless moments where surrender seemed like the only option, yet an inexplicable force propelled me to rise once more. Each setback, each trial, became a lesson in fortitude, teaching me that resilience is less about bouncing back and more about evolving with each blow.

In the darkest hours, when despair threatened to engulf every glimmer of hope, resilience manifested as a quiet determination. It whispered that this too shall pass, that the scars borne from these battles would one day tell a story of survival and strength. It is in these moments that I found the courage to navigate through the storm, to seek out the faintest light in the abyss, and to hold onto it with unwavering tenacity.

The legacy of resilience is not only a personal testament but also a beacon for others who grapple with their own adversities. I have come to understand that sharing these stories of struggle and triumph can ignite a spark of hope in those who feel trapped in their own darkness. The narrative of resilience serves as a reminder that we are not defined by the hardships we face, but by how we choose to confront and transcend them.

In the quiet reflection of these experiences, I am reminded of the power of perspective. It is often said that adversity reveals true character, but I believe it also reveals the boundless potential within us. The challenges that once seemed insurmountable now stand as milestones of growth, each one contributing to a reservoir of inner strength that continues to expand.

Resilience has also taught me the importance of compassion—towards oneself and others. In the process of overcoming my own struggles, I have learned to extend grace to those who are fighting their battles. The empathy born from shared experiences creates a web of support, where each thread of resilience intertwines, offering solace and encouragement.

As I navigate through life, I carry with me the lessons imparted by adversity. The resilience that has been nurtured through these trials is a testament to the human spirit's capacity for endurance and transformation. It serves as a constant reminder that while we cannot always control the circumstances we face, we possess the power to shape our response.

In the end, resilience is not a destination but a continuous journey of growth and self-discovery. It is the quiet strength that propels us forward, the unwavering belief that we can weather any storm. It is the legacy that adversity bequeaths, a gift that, while hard-earned, becomes the foundation upon which we build our lives.

FINAL REFLECTIONS

As I sit back and ponder the multitude of experiences chronicled in this book, my mind swirls with a kaleidoscope of emotions. Each chapter, each story, is not just a recounting of events but a profound exploration of the human spirit. The trials and tribulations faced were not mere obstacles but transformative experiences that shaped the essence of who I am today. The pages of this book don't just tell a story; they reflect a journey of growth, resilience, and self-discovery.

Life's adversities, as daunting as they may seem, often serve as the crucible in which our true character is forged. When faced with seemingly insurmountable challenges, it's easy to succumb to despair. However, the moments of darkness also hold the potential for the greatest light. Each setback encountered was an opportunity to dig deeper, to find strength in places I never thought to look. The process was neither linear nor predictable, but it was undeniably enriching.

Reflecting on the myriad of lessons learned, one stands out with striking clarity: the power of perspective. Changing how I viewed my circumstances transformed my reality. What once seemed like an unyielding barrier became a stepping stone to greater understanding and compassion. This shift in perspective did not come easily. It required a deliberate and often painful effort to see beyond the immediate discomfort and envision a broader horizon.

The people who walked alongside me during these times also played an indispensable role. Their support, empathy, and sometimes tough love were the anchors that kept me grounded. These relationships, forged in the fires of adversity, are some of the most profound connections I have ever known. They taught me the invaluable lesson that vulnerability is not a weakness, but a strength. Allowing myself to lean on others opened the door to deeper, more meaningful interactions.

Resilience is a word often thrown around, but its true essence is felt only when tested. The capacity to bounce back, to rise after falling, is not an innate trait but a learned skill. Through each story shared in this book, the underlying theme is one of resilience honed through experience. It is the quiet, persistent strength that emerges when all else seems lost. It is the whisper of hope that refuses to be silenced.

Looking back, it is evident that adversity is not something to be feared or avoided, but rather, embraced as an integral part of the human experience. It is through these challenges that the most significant growth occurs. Each scar, each wound, tells a story of survival and triumph. The journey through adversity is not just about overcoming obstacles but about becoming a better, more empathetic, and understanding person.

In writing this book, my aim was not just to share my personal experiences but to offer a beacon of hope to those navigating their own struggles. If there is one takeaway, it is that adversity, while painful, is also a powerful catalyst for change and growth. The human spirit is remarkably resilient, capable of enduring and thriving despite the most challenging circumstances. As I close this chapter, I do so with a heart full of gratitude and a spirit fortified by the lessons learned along the way.

THE JOURNEY CONTINUES

Life has a peculiar way of teaching us lessons, often when we least expect them. Reflecting on the path I have walked, I see a tapestry woven with threads of hardship and triumph. Each challenge, each obstacle, has been a chapter in the story of my personal growth. Moments of despair have given birth to resilience, transforming adversity into a powerful catalyst for change.

As I look back, I recall the times when I felt overwhelmed by the weight of my struggles. It was during these moments that I discovered the depths of my own strength. The support of loved ones, the kindness of strangers, and the unexpected opportunities that arose from seemingly insurmountable problems all contributed to my evolving perspective. Through these experiences, I have learned that every setback carries within it the seeds of opportunity.

The lessons I have learned are not just about overcoming difficulties but also about understanding myself better. There were times when I questioned my own abilities, doubted my worth, and felt lost in the chaos of life's challenges. Yet, it was through these very doubts that I found clarity. I learned to trust my instincts, to value my own voice, and to recognize the importance of self-compassion.

Understanding that adversity is an inevitable part of life has been a crucial realization. It is not the absence of difficulties that defines us, but rather how we respond to them. Adopting a mindset that sees obstacles as opportunities for growth has transformed my approach to life's challenges. This shift in perspective has allowed me to face difficulties with a sense of curiosity rather than fear, seeing them as puzzles to be solved rather than insurmountable barriers.

In this ongoing journey, I have also come to appreciate the importance of gratitude. Even in the darkest of times, there are moments of light, however small they may seem. A kind word from a friend, a beautiful sunset, or a quiet moment of reflection can provide the strength needed to keep moving forward. Cultivating gratitude has been a powerful tool in maintaining a positive outlook, helping me to focus on what I have rather than what I lack.

The path ahead remains uncertain, as it always has been. But with each step, I feel more equipped to handle whatever comes my way. The experiences that once felt like burdens have become sources of wisdom and strength. They remind me that I am capable, that I am resilient, and that I am constantly growing.

Life's challenges have taught me to be patient with myself, to celebrate small victories, and to view each day as an opportunity to learn and evolve. As I continue to navigate through the ups and downs, I hold on to the belief that every experience, no matter how difficult, contributes to my personal growth.

Reflecting on my journey, I see a story of transformation. Adversity has not only tested my limits but has also expanded them. It has shown me the power of perseverance, the importance of self-belief, and the beauty of resilience. Each step forward is a testament to the strength that lies within, a reminder that every challenge faced is a step towards becoming the best version of myself.